SUCCESSFULLY
IMPLEMENTING
ERP
SECOND EDITION

A GUIDE FOR SMB OWNERS AND EXECUTIVES

SYLVAIN LAFOND

Leaders Press

Leaders
Press

ISBN 978-1-63735-231-1 (pbk)
ISBN 978-1-63735-230-4 (ebook)

Library of Congress Control Number 2023906565

UPGRADE YOUR ERP KNOWLEDGE WITH A FREE 2-HOUR WEBINAR!

AS A SPECIAL THANK-YOU TO OUR FIRST HUNDRED BUYERS OF SUCCESSFULLY IMPLEMENTING ERP, SECOND EDITION, WE'RE EXCITED TO OFFER A FREE 2-HOUR WEBINAR. OUR EXPERT PANEL INCLUDES INDUSTRY LEADERS IN CYBERSECURITY, E-COMMERCE, CHANGE MANAGEMENT, BUSINESS INTELLIGENCE, AND OF COURSE, ERP SYSTEMS. LED BY AUTHOR SLY, THIS LIVE Q&A SESSION WILL ENHANCE YOUR ERP KNOWLEDGE AND OPEN THE DOOR TO NEW OPPORTUNITIES AND POSSIBILITIES.

DON'T MISS OUT ON THIS VALUABLE OPPORTUNITY TO UPGRADE YOUR ERP GAME.

SECURE YOUR SPOT AT THE UPCOMING WEBINAR BY VISITING ERPHELP.CO TODAY!

ERPHELP.CO

Reading Lafond's book feels like having a coffee chat with a genius friend – 'Successfully Implementing ERP' is the game plan every SMB owner craves.

Jonathan Barriault, ing., MBA, PMP | Former ERP Selection Consultant for GLM Conseils

Sylvain Lafond's guide isn't just a book; it's a magic wand for SMBs – 'Successfully Implementing ERP' transforms your business challenges into opportunities effortlessly.

Aime-Christian Hakizimana | Sr Account Executive at SherWeb

Successfully Implementing ERP explains in clear, concise language how to smoothly integrate ERP software into your business operations. Industry veteran Sylvain Lafond, draws on his extensive experience as an ERP consultant to walk readers through the process of planning, executing and optimizing an ERP implementation as effectively—and efficiently—as possible.

Hassan El-Asmar | Controller at Logix ITS

In a world of ERP confusion, Sylvain Lafond is the lighthouse guiding SMBs to clarity – 'Successfully Implementing ERP' is the light every business needs.

Gilles Croteau | CFO at Protech Chemicals

A must-have for SMB executives! Sylvain Lafond's 'Successfully Implementing ERP' is a gem. The book's focus on real-world case studies and industry-specific insights sets it apart. Lafond's expertise is evident, making this a game-changing resource for small and medium-sized businesses.

Philippe Palmarini | Former IT Direct at Solmax International, Current Customer Care Administrator & Consultant at Vokeso

Successfully Implementing ERP' is a comprehensive guide that speaks directly to the challenges faced by small and medium-sized businesses. Lafond's expertise shines through every page.

James Lapalme | Professor, Ecole de technologie superieure.

I'm no tech wizard, but Lafond's book made ERP sound like a piece of cake – 'Successfully Implementing ERP' is the cheat code for SMB success.

Gilles Bléfari | Mentor & Former IT consultant

TABLE OF CONTENTS

PREFACE

Stories are a communal currency of humanity.
—Tahir Shah, author of *In Arabian Nights*

In the preface of the first edition, I applauded how Sylvain managed to cover the vast and complex terrain that is ERP implementation in a manner that is simple but not overly simplistic. In this new edition, Sylvain brings a new dimension to the book: humanity.

This edition offers narratives that explain the process of implementing an ERP system through human experience. The narratives anchor the rest of the book to make technical jargon resonate with the daily experiences of business owners.

This edition also covers more territory by expanding the number of topics that are covered, hence making it more relevant in the context of key technologies that business owners should consider.

I really hope you enjoy this little gem.

Sincerely,
James Lapalme, P.Eng, PhD,
Professor at École de technologie supérieure,
Montréal, 2023

(I did not remunerate James to write this preface. As you might guess, there are other considerations involved. Friendship is one. Hubris probably is another. Nah, just kidding. It's all about friendship, and board gaming experience is our currency.)

ACKNOWLEDGMENT

People who uplift you are the best kind of people.
You don't simply keep them. You have to treasure
them.

—Dodinsky

> **Key Takeaway: I did not do this all by myself.**

As Margaret Cousins so eloquently put it, "Appreciation can make a day, even change a life. Your willingness to put it into words is all that is necessary." The support and help I have received from all the people below made the writing of this book not only possible but also enjoyable. I hereby take the time necessary to express my gratitude and put it all into words.

I must begin by thanking Kristen Hernandez and the good people at Leaders Press. Their expertise, professionalism, and constant effort provided me with a steady influx of energy. Kristen's upbeat attitude was contagious. Leaders Press challenged me and was instrumental in making this book much better than the first edition. I think. I suppose. I hope.

They say, "Behind every great man is a great woman." I say, "Don't wait too long before bringing it up." Nathalie has been by my side for a few precious years now, and I cannot imagine where I would be without her continuous support, patience, and insight. She is a truly exceptional individual, and I am privileged to share my life with her. How can you find fault with someone who introduced you to sailing?

As I continue sprinkling my gratitude, next comes James Lapalme. He is a board-gaming friend who happens to hold a PhD in my field of expertise. He provided great insight and was kind enough to write the preface to this book (*again*). He is also magnanimous enough to let me occasionally beat him at board games, which greatly elevates my ego. He may not realize how important his involvement has been for me.

My team at Vokeso has also been a great help. This second edition will benefit from its own website with content specifically created for you, the reader. Special thanks to Alexandra Barci Tessier, Yassine Ben Ammar, Marco Chartier, Abhilasha Dasgupta, Alex Ngu, Frédéric Légaré, and Gianclaudio Oliveira, among others for their efforts.

Finally, there are other people who have been there for me along the path. I would like to thank each and every one of them but will refrain from doing so lest this book turns into another genealogical litany like *The Silmarillion*, written by J. R. R. Tolkien, or the more familiar book of Genesis. They know who they are.

INTRODUCTION

We read to know we are not alone.

—C. S. Lewis

Key Takeaway: You are not alone anymore!

If you just downloaded and *opened* this book (*and you are not my editor or a member of my family*), then I hope you are looking for some help with your enterprise resource planning (ERP) system. All the better if you are not yet using an ERP system but are looking into deploying one.

This book is not *ERP for Dummies.* You are not stupid. You are most likely a business owner or an executive trying to make sense of this jungle that is the ERP industry. This may even be your first brush with these new acronyms and concepts, and a little help would come in handy. If you are not even sure what ERP stands for, think CRM is some kind of car part, or are wondering why people keep talking about clouds all the time, no worries, we have you covered.

The first edition of this book, already dating back to 2018, was written to help decision-makers looking to buy and deploy an ERP system make sense of the process. *(It was also written to bolster my ego, but that didn't work, as the number of reviews on Amazon. ca will attest.)*

This second edition has been updated to reflect the latest tendencies—and because five years is an eternity where technology and information systems are concerned.

The objective of *Successfully Implementing ERP* remains the same: assisting you in understanding the challenges you face and helping you prepare accordingly. Ultimately, our greatest hope is to support you in making the right decisions for a successful project.

Please keep in mind that this guide is meant as a good overview. You do not have time to read 547 pages, and you do not need to teach the topic. You simply need to understand it sufficiently to steer your organization in the right direction and get it the solution it requires.

This second edition still contains short chapters with witty quotes, examples, and a key takeaway, but a new narrative section has been added to make this a little bit more fun and concrete. *(Talking about fun, I've also taken the liberty of sharing some of my inner thoughts, here and there, attempting to be funny. You let me know if I should keep my day job.)*

These new short stories should help make some of the most important concepts more palatable. The objective is for you, the reader, to recognize or imagine yourself in some of these situations such that you can learn from them—despite knowing they are, obviously, pure fiction. Or are they?

You will also find this work salted with illustrations and sweetened with a touch of humor. ERP may be boring and challenging to many, but reading this book does not have to make you feel like you are perusing a corporate tax guide!

I also want to point out that the sequence of chapters is not indicative of the sequence in which you need to follow the steps in order to select or implement an ERP system. Some steps may be omitted or performed in a different order. For example, a *request for information* may be appropriate in providing valuable information needed to flesh out your *business case*.

Today, numerous solutions exist on the market, addressing the needs of small and large companies in almost any industry. Options abound, and with all these options, confusion arises. Please read on as we explore the ramifications and challenges of selecting and deploying integrated management systems.

One more note before you get going: the business cases presented in this book are mostly inspired by true stories, but as the motion-picture series *Dragnet* said it:

"Ladies and gentlemen: the story you are about to hear is true. Only the names have been changed to protect the innocent."

SECTION 1

HAPPENSTANCE

A Chance Encounter at the Gym

For the past two winters, Benjamin had been spending multiple weeks in St. Martin, teleworking, with his spouse, Elizabeth. This had given them the opportunity to run away from the @$%& cold and white $#!T of their province of residence: Quebec. It had also provided additional benefits, such as taking a few days off or finding a gym where he could work out regularly. This was made possible and worthwhile because of their lengthy stay.

Ben had been a regular at the gym, and it showed. He was of average height, but his frame exuded power, as is often the case with people who work out regularly. Despite a slightly severe look with his shaved head and goatee, his sparkling brown eyes, big smile, and a good sense of humor still made him likable.

He really enjoyed working at GymFit. The physical exertion helped balance the intellectual demands of his job as an ERP consultant, something he had been doing well for nearly twenty years. He also believed that taking care of oneself involved focusing on all four aspects of a person—spiritual, emotional, intellectual, and of course, physical.

As he finished his last set of curls, he noticed there was someone using the lat pulldown machine, his next workstation. A tall, lean but muscular, well-groomed man with blue eyes and blond hair.

Benjamin was an easygoing guy with a well-honed ability to make himself known. It came with the territory as a consultant. So he walked over to the machine and introduced himself to the gentleman exercising there, asking if they could share and alternate their sets. He was expecting him to respond with a French accent, or perhaps a response in English, but it turned out the gentleman was also a French Canadian guy called...Guy.

As they were taking turns performing their sets, Ben tried to make conversation:

"So, Guy, where are you from?"

"Montreal North Shore. Laval, to be exact," responded Guy.

"Interesting. I'm from the South Shore myself," said Ben with a smile. "Is it your first trip to Saint Martin?"

"Yup," answered Guy. "Please give me a minute to do my reps," continued Guy as he positioned himself and grabbed the pulley bar.

"Sure, sorry," interjected Ben. He inwardly counted fifteen reps. "Thanks. My turn now," said Ben as Guy removed himself from the bench.

Ben counted his eight reps. Guy respectfully waited for Ben, diverting himself by looking around at the other people activating themselves around the gym.

"You'll see it's a great island," continued Ben after his set was finished. "We fell in love with it a few years ago, my girlfriend and I. Every winter, we visit for as many weeks as we can. People are friendly, the beaches are nice, and there's very good dining."

"Looking forward to it!" said Guy. "We're here for a week, my wife and I." Guy took his seat.

Ben mentally counted Guy's fifteen reps again and then asked, as he was taking his turn, "Where are you staying?"

While Ben performed his reps, Guy handled the conversation:

"We rented a condo in Orient Bay. Through Airbnb. It's just a short drive from here. You know where that is?"

"Uuurgh," answered Ben, and then he got to eight. "Yes," Ben said, panting. "We are also staying in that area. Why don't we get together tonight for a drink? We could meet at the Bikini."

"The what?" said Guy.

"The Bikini Beach," answered Benjamin. "It's not far from the String. I kid you not," he added, laughing, "that's what these places are called. The String is great, but it only opens for lunch."

"All right. Seven o'clock tonight?" asked Guy.

"That should work," replied Ben. "Just give me your phone number in case Beth has booked us on something else. If you don't hear from me in a few hours, then we're on!"

They proceeded to exchange phone numbers and, after a friendly fist bump, continued their workout, going separate ways to complete their routine.

An Evening at the Bikini

That same evening, Benjamin and Elizabeth were using the sidewalks, meandering through the condo buildings on their way to the beach from where they would walk a short distance to the Bikini Beach Restaurant. The terraced restaurant—with its bar, patios, and wooden furniture—was right on the beach. It offered a nice view of the Atlantic Ocean and the islands of Pinel and Tintamarre.

There they met with Guy, who waved them over, and his spouse, Linda. They sat down, ordered drinks, and soon got involved in discussions about St. Martin, their lives, their families, and various other topics that people broach when getting to know each other.

Predictably, the discussion eventually turned to work. Linda was a teacher, Elizabeth a lawyer. Benjamin asked Guy about his professional life:

"And you, Guy, what do you do?"

"I'm the IT director at Thingamajig Manufacturers Inc.," proudly answered Guy.

"That's a good job. Usually very demanding though," added Ben, showing a touch of concern to show Guy he was actively listening and to keep him engaged in the conversation.

"Yes, especially nowadays as we are trying to install a new system."

"What kind of system? If you're allowed to say, of course," inquired Ben.

"Sure, it's no secret. We are installing a new ERP. Have you heard of that before?"

Following a spontaneous laugh, Benjamin replied, "Oh yeah! It's what I do for a living. I'm an ERP specialist."

"No shit!" exclaimed Guy. "What a coincidence. What do you do exactly? Maybe you could help me."

To which Ben replied, "I work for Vokeso, a Microsoft partner. We specialize in selling and implementing business solutions. Our main thing is Dynamics 365 Business Central. My official title is director of operations, but my real job is peeing on fires and making sure everyone is happy." He added, laughing, "Seriously, my role is to supervise the specialists who work with our clients. I oversee the team and the various projects we deliver."

"So you've done implementations before," confirmed Guy.

"Quite a few, yes. This is how I got started in the business."

At that point, Beth and Linda started their own discussion, as if they could sense where this was going, particularly Linda, and that it would very quickly become boring as hell.

"All right! Do you mind if I tell you about what's going on back at the office? Perhaps you can share your thoughts?" probed Guy.

"Sure, go ahead," graciously offered Ben.

"Thanks!" You could sense the enthusiasm in Guy for having found a good ear and for the opportunity to tell his story. "The owner of the company, Claudia, made the decision last year to buy an ERP system. We hired a consulting firm to help us select a solution that would work for us. We revised and documented our processes, identified our requirements, attended demonstrations, and ultimately selected a solution. I suppose this is pretty standard stuff," posited Guy as he paused to be reassured that their process had been sound.

"It is. Whenever a company hires a selection consultant." He then proceeded to explain, "The process can be slightly different in other situations. Businesses that do this work themselves, for instance, don't always go into as many details, and it can shorten the whole exercise."

"Ah, okay. So I guess I shouldn't be too concerned that this took five months then."

"No, that would be normal."

"That makes me feel better," continued Guy. "After the paperwork was done, we put a team together. Some of our people and some of our vendor's consultants would make up the project team. They also assigned a project manager, and the owner gave me the internal project manager job. We had to do this, apparently, and I think she trusts me."

Ben validated this approach by saying, "This all sounds appropriate."

Seeming quite thoughtful and concerned following that statement, Guy went on to explain the first few steps of the project: The project started after the holidays. A kick-off meeting was followed by a business review conducted by the consultants. Then they had workshops to learn the solution, discuss configuration options, and test various use cases.

The mood was generally optimistic during these first few months, and progress seemed steady enough. Sure, they had some obstacles and issues to circumvent, but ultimately, they were able to resolve them with discussions and meetings.

Some necessary customizations were identified during the workshops. The consultants documented the functional gaps, and most were approved by the steering committee. While their vendor delegated this extra work to their technical team, the pace slowed a bit, but the rest of the team dedicated themselves to writing user guides, preparing data, and documenting the various tests they would perform during the integrated testing phase. That phase was supposed to be performed once everything was ready and they returned to full staff after the summer months.

"I see. Again, nothing strange here. But you seem concerned, Guy. What happened next?"

"Well, that's when poo started hitting the fan," replied Guy emotionally. Evidently, he cared much about this project he was involved in and seemed to almost take it personally if they were having problems. "First, in August, when all this programming work was getting done, one of my key people from the purchasing department went on sick leave. Almost at the same time, one of the vendor's consultants quit his job. We liked the guy. He was really good."

"Were these people replaced?"

"Yes and no. We pulled someone else from the same department to replace the lady who went on leave, but that new person had so much to learn. She needed time to get up to speed. On top of that, she kept rescheduling meetings and missing deadlines. Everything crawled to a near halt with that department.

"Since our vendor could not find a quick replacement for the manufacturing consultant who left, the project manager took on the load as soon as he got back from his summer vacation. I think he is overwhelmed though."

"Yeah. Not an ideal situation," confirmed Ben.

To which Guy added emphatically, "Indeed. To add insult to injury, we were hacked at the beginning of September, so I had to spend nearly a month on this new problem. I couldn't really take care of the project during that time."

"Wow!" interjected Ben with an honest dose of compassion. "How did you end up getting through this?"

"By working my ass off. The hackers wanted bitcoins, of course. We decided not to pay, but that meant wiping our machines, reinstalling everything from scratch, and restoring as much data as we could from backups. A nightmare!"

"I'm sorry you had to go through this," said Ben with sympathy. "I know a good company that can help you with cybersecurity in the future, if you ever want to talk to them."

"Thanks, man, I appreciate it." Guy really seemed to find relief by being able to share his tribulations with Ben, and he told him as much before continuing his horror story:

"We were supposed to perform integrated testing during the fall, but of course, none of that happened. The developers took longer than expected to write our custom code, and by the time they were ready, it was almost Christmas.

"Still, we started testing what had been done, and some of our users were complaining that not everything was as it should be. Particularly our controller. He is part of the steering committee and an important project sponsor, but he has been very vocal about his loss of control, that he can't see any benefit and we'll never have the ease of use of the old system. Moreover, he tells anyone who will listen that this was a mistake and that we will never implement. According to him, this project is bound to fail.

"The owner has decided to pause the project and reevaluate. We had a huge argument, she and I, in January about this, and that's when I decided to take a break and go on vacation. You see why I am so discouraged with this project? I am even considering tending my resignation when I get back."

"Hm. Okay, I understand," said Ben. "And again, I feel for you. Some of what you have been going through is not unheard of. I have seen this happen before. But having all this occur on the same project is a bit exceptional. Especially your controller freaking out like that. Accounting is a finite science, and usually, this is not the department from where the most resistance emanates."

"Listen," continued Ben after a short pause. "There is much to discuss, and it is getting late. Why don't we continue this chat later? I want to think about everything you told me and maybe provide some ideas. For now, I'd say don't consider quitting just yet. Let's see what we can come up with."

"That would be awesome. But I don't want to impose on your vacation time. I mean, this is bothering me to no end, but it is not your problem." To which he added conspicuously, "Even Linda is getting kind of fed up with me talking about this all the time, and I think she'd be happy to see me quit."

"No worries," Ben said with a sheepish smile. "Since it is not happening to me, I am removed enough, so it becomes an interesting challenge." He turned to Elizabeth and teasingly told her, "Honey, should we not head back to the condo while you can still stand?"

A Day in the Life

The following morning, Benjamin was sitting outside on a chair with his laptop in front of him on a small round table. The day was sunny, slightly windy, and simply gorgeous, as were most days in St. Martin. He was teleconferencing his weekly operations meeting with the various department supervisors.

"Team, let me start today's meeting by sharing a little story. There was an earthquake last night! I'm serious. I was awakened at three a.m. The bed was shaking and rattling against the wall." He quickly caught himself and said, "Please let's not go there. Elizabeth was in the bathroom, and we were both wondering what was going on. I looked for information on my phone, and it appears it was a four-point-nine tremor on the Richter scale, about a hundred miles off the coast."

"Wow! Were you scared?" asked Thomas, the technical supervisor.

"Not really. It was over quickly, and by the time we figured out what it was, it was too late anyway," said Ben, laughing.

Most of the group joined in the laughter.

"Well, I guess this is going to be your last trip to St. Martin. You know we can't afford to lose you," joked Helen, who worked in administration.

"Ha! Very funny. Not happening. So let's move on to the serious stuff now," said Ben. "First, please remember that we are approaching the month end and all time sheets must be in on time. You know how Helen gets when she has to herd sheep and invoicing gets delayed," he added as he winked at her, effectively winking at everybody as he was facing a computer screen.

To which Helen retorted, with her usual sense of humor, "Guys, just make sure your people don't have a knitting class taking up too much of their precious time so they can enter their time sheets. Thanks."

After everyone nodded their approval or rolled their eyes at the nth reminder, Benjamin asked if anyone had an issue they needed addressed. The first portion of their weekly meeting was always spent trying to identify and correct issues for customers, especially issues that required interdepartmental involvement.

Bao, whose new role as supervisor of the customer care department put him in front of problems all the time, raised his yellow virtual hand in Teams.

"You got the floor, Bao," said Benjamin.

"Thank you. I want to bring up a concern a customer voiced yesterday. He needs a new report, and the tech department gave me an estimate of two to three days. The client is freaking out. He says it's only a few columns and it would probably take him less than a day to put together in Excel. Thom tells me he trusts his developer's estimate. Still, I don't understand how to justify it to the customer."

"Yeah. Good one," replied Ben. "Programming is not easy. Be kind to your programmers. In my first year of college, there were one hundred ten students enrolled in the program, twenty-seven graduated three years later. It takes a special breed of people to code." He went on, "The blunt truth is that most customers are not competent enough to evaluate our work. You don't see me telling my mechanic how to replace the brakes on my car. They don't understand what's involved. Comparing Excel to Business Central, you know," said Ben, shrugging in resignation.

"How about having their former project manager give them a call? Just to reassure them?" asked Carla, the implementation supervisor.

"Good idea," replied Bao with some enthusiasm. "I will reach out to you today to discuss the details. Thanks!"

"Please make sure we communicate to the customer that we are not in the business of swindling them. Or anyone else for that matter. We will only invoice the time we spend, not one penny more," demanded Benjamin. "One other thing," he added. "Invite them to a meeting with the developer so he can show them the actual complexity involved. We have nothing to hide."

"Will do!" assured Carla.

"All right. Next problem?" inquired Ben.

"Me, me, pick me!" said Carla. They all had a good laugh at that *Shrek* reference. Once the order was brought back to the meeting, Carla was able to expose her problem:

"As you know, Ahmed is soon leaving on paternity leave. The poor guy decided to have a kid. Well, it's his wife, but you know what I mean. I told him not to make that mistake. I'd know, I have four myself. He didn't listen," complained Clara with cynical humor.

"No one does," confirmed Helen, always ready to participate.

"Well, he will be away for six weeks. He's currently working on only one project, but he was about to start training super users. I need someone to jump in, but my entire team is tapped. I thought about borrowing someone from Bao's team or perhaps even someone in Thom's department. What do you guys think?"

"I would do it in a heartbeat," said Bao, "but we're falling behind on support tickets."

"Thom?" asked Ben. "Anyone with the ability to help in your department?"

"Maybe," hesitantly responded Thomas. "I have to pick someone with enough functional experience to teach, preferably someone with a consultant certification. It also has to be someone comfortable enough to do this. Someone with the right people skills. Let me talk to my team, Carla. I will get back to you."

"Okay. Thanks, Thom," she replied. "I appreciate it."

"Anyone else?" asked Ben.

"Me again," said Carla. "I think we may be having some problems with our estimates in presales. We recently blew up the development budget on a couple of projects. On one project for Tremblay and Son Inc., we had to customize for special invoicing requirements. The other project at Making Things LLC needed an integration between Business Central and some design or manufacturing platform. I forget the name."

"Yeah," emphasized Thom. "The work was much more complex than what we first thought."

"Did you help Sam with his estimates?" asked Ben. Sam was the presales consultant responsible for demonstrations, proposals, and ultimately, closing new business.

"Yes, we did," answered Thom. "With the information Sam provided at the time. But it seems that when Carla's team started working with the customers, after they signed, to analyze and flesh out the work, everything got out of hand and became way more complicated."

"Hmm. Is it possible that the information Sam received was not detailed enough?" questioned Ben. "I have certainly seen this before. Hell is in the details, as we say."

"Clearly," answered Thom. "In the invoicing case, there was a specific tracking requirement that we had to address by creating a new ledger in the system. That was never brought up before. It was something we did not see coming despite being given process flows by the customer."

"Ah! That makes sense," reflected Ben. "It's so hard in presales to anticipate and properly evaluate all the gaps. On top of that, we don't yet fully understand the customer's business, and they don't know BC. It's about not knowing what we don't know, if you know what I mean. What are we doing to help the customer in this case?"

Carla answered, "We are reducing our rate."

"The client is happy with this?" Ben asked.

"It seems so," answered Clara, "but we better get this finished soon."

"All right, keep me posted please," concluded Ben. "What about the integration?"

"Well, this one's messy," responded Thom. "Besides waiting on the other vendor for answers and the web services they promised, we are also finding out new transactions and data needing to be exchanged almost daily. Somebody really didn't think this one through."

Benjamin emitted a long sigh this time. "Can you and Carla please look at the documentation, what was promised and what's been done so far? I will talk to Sam to find out what happened upstream. Eighty percent of our problems are always communication problems. If we screwed up, we may need to eat our socks on this one."

"When are you meeting with him?" asked Carla.

"Later this week. Thursday, I think," answered Ben. "I'll keep you posted."

They nodded their agreement.

The meeting went on like this for some time.

"Anything else?" inquired Ben. When no one came forward, he added, "Okay, I have an issue. I just want to reiterate the importance of following our methodology. Taking the time to properly document and communicate could save us from hassles like this integration problem we just talked about. Even more so with all this remote work we're doing. I am not saying we're failing here, but I just want to make sure you keep applying pressure on your teams so we stay on track. Sound good?"

"Will do!" assured Carla.

Once the pressing issues were addressed, Ben said, "Good. Let's review the projects now. Carla, can you lead us through this please?"

Carla proceeded to enumerate the list of ongoing projects, and for each one, they made sure that there were no major stumbling blocks, that they were on time, and that resources were properly allocated. Nobody's perfect, but the management team was highly motivated to keep all projects under control, which meant controlling the budget, the timeline, and the scope. This effort was genuine but of limited impact as much of the responsibility lay with the customers.

The meeting went on like this for some time before the group's focus turned to their quarterly rocks. The quarterly rocks were named this way in honor of the frequently used metaphor for prioritization: trying to fit big rocks, pebbles, and then sand into an empty jar. The jar represents your life, and the big rocks represent the most important priorities.

Having gone through the EOS (Entrepreneurial Operating System™), whereby a company's vision is defined before any traction can manifest itself, they had adopted the meeting tools used to keep track of the most important goals and activities of the company. This was how most weekly operational meetings went.

As much fun as it was, Benjamin could not help but anticipate the end of the day. This was the time when he could explore the island while St. Martin delivered on its promises. After all, it was the Friendly Island.

The Gastronomical Capital of the Caribbean

Following their first evening together, the two couples had spent some time at the Orient Bay Beach and had even visited the island of Saint Barthelemy together, which they accessed via ferry. The temperature was warm, but the weather was uncharacteristically windy for this time of year. The forty-five-minute crossing was somewhat choppy, and Guy had even been slightly indisposed.

Despite that, spending a day driving around the hilly island together, beach-hopping, and exploring the gorgeous neighborhoods was momentous. They were getting along quite well, so much so that they had decided to dine together the next day. Elizabeth had been able to make reservations at Le Pressoir, their favorite restaurant on the island. Le Pressoir, French fine dining at its best, was located in the gastronomical capital of St. Martin: Grand Case.

On the following evening, the two couples were sitting at a table on the terrace overlooking the Grand Case boulevard, sipping a cocktail. They were getting along quite well. While Elizabeth and Linda were involved in a lively discussion about their work, the men turned their attention to Guy's ERP implementation problems.

Benjamin started the discussion by reassuring Guy that he had given his predicament some thought. He went on to provide some advice:

"Listen," he said, "don't take everything I say as gospel. Every situation is unique, and we are dealing with people. You know your folks better than me. Still, it seems to me you are facing a breach of confidence, right?"

"Yes," agreed Guy.

"Okay. Firstly, don't take it personally. Change is hard, and most people aren't comfortable when they perceive they are losing control. In reality, we don't control much, but most people prefer to ignore this truth.

"Secondly, no one is a prophet in their own country. You may want to consider hiring a consultant to perform an assessment and make recommendations. In the end, he may reach the same conclusions as you, but having someone from the outside say it can add credibility and weight."

"I guess that makes sense," pondered Guy.

They were interrupted by the owner of the restaurant serving their appetizers. *La bisque de langouste* (lobster bisque), *l'œuf parfait* (egg perfect), and *le foie gras fusion caraibes* had all been selected. They were distributed around the table—all delectable dishes requiring their full attention and way too good to allow conversation.

Following this incredible opening, discussions resumed while they were waiting for their main dish. They had all chosen the St. Martin menu based on local produce, and it comprised three services.

Guy, curious to hear more, prodded Benjamin for more counsel.

"Okay. So another thing I would recommend is for you to get help with project management. If you want to continue running this project yourself, then get help with your regular department tasks. If you want to relaunch this project and take it to the finish line, you will need to be on top of it, a hundred and ten percent."

Guy was nodding emphatically.

"Now, here's a tough one. The assessment will probably reveal, as you mentioned, that you are almost there. Chances are your boss... what was her name again?"

"Claudia," answered Guy.

"Right, Claudia. She should realize it doesn't make sense to waste all the money and resources already invested. At that point, she should agree to restart. That's good, but you need, *absolutely need*," Ben insisted, "to get her on board. This project needs her positive leadership. Find a way, with the help of your consultant, to make her commit to that role. A project like this is too important to deprive it of top leadership. Everyone in the organization needs to know how big this is and that Claudia is behind it."

"Woah. That may not be easy," stated Guy.

"I know," answered Ben. "But this is your biggest challenge. You need to make this happen somehow."

After a pause, Benjamin added, "Here's a suggestion. If Claudia had a chance to talk to other executives about their experience with ERP deployments, she might be reassured that what happened is not unheard of."

"That's a good idea. Claudia is a member of an organization called Entrechefs. I will suggest she brings this up when she attends the next event," concluded Guy.

"Once that's accomplished," Benjamin continued, "get everyone involved. Every single employee needs to know what happened and what you've learned. Let them know what you've decided to do and how you are going to do it. Finally, make sure you establish a two-way feedback channel between the project team and the employees. Keep them informed throughout the project, and listen to them. You may need to comfort some of them from time to time, or they may come up with great ideas about issues and opportunities for improvement.

"That's why I need help," reflected Guy. "This is a lot of work."

"Yup!" answered Ben. "Saddle up, my friend," he added, laughing. "Also, I am assuming that your business processes have been documented properly. If that's not the case, be ready to review and challenge them."

At that moment, their waiter arrived with the main course. Ben had ordered *le medaillon de langouste*, Guy and Elizabeth received their *supreme de volaille*, while Linda had ordered *la pluma ibérique*. They ate their meals with gusto, and the conversation forked toward mundane topics.

After some tasty dessert, they left the restaurant with the owner Gil's good wishes and decided to walk up and down Grand Case Boulevard to check out the boutiques and get a good dose of the Caribbean vibes.

The Challenges of Selling

On Thursday, as planned, Benjamin and Sam faced one another in their weekly sales meeting. After the usual formalities, Benjamin decided to start the meeting with the delicate subject of the integration going bad at Making Things Inc.

For something like this, he had prepared a communication vector—a concept he had learned in his communication training provided by a local company called Psycom.

"Sam, in my operations meeting earlier this week, the topic of Making Things Inc. was brought up." He could already notice Sam tensing, so he decided to slow things down a little and slightly alter his original vector.

The first component of a vector is the context. As such, it is often the lengthiest part of the message, and therefore, it seemed fine to add some content to it.

"The team shared their concern with me and made it clear that you followed the proper steps during the presales process."

With that statement, Sam eased up a bit.

Benjamin continued, "It appears that despite analyzing the integration requirements and asking the technical department to get involved, we misjudged the body of work needed to get this done. My immediate concern, as you might guess, is the well-being of the project."

Just as Sam was about to interject, Ben raised his hand to indicate that he was not finished. "However," he plodded on, "I am also preoccupied with our methods and their efficacy. Are we being blindsided by some defect in our procedures?" Without waiting for an answer, he added, "I need your help, Sam, to figure this out. I would like to conduct a postmortem sometime soon with you and Carla if you don't mind."

Benjamin stopped and relaxed, clearly indicating to Sam that it was his turn to share his thoughts.

"I agree, Ben," answered Sam. "I am also concerned, and I have had some discussions with the client to appease them and try to figure out what is going wrong. They agree it's not entirely our fault. It seems one of their main developers has much knowledge in his head and is feeling threatened. As such, he may not have disclosed enough information to help us with our initial analysis."

"Interesting," reflected Ben. "This reassures me a little."

"I still feel we could have done more," said Sam. "I have a hunch we were blindsided because we were too trusting or maybe not pushy enough."

"Thanks for your input, Sam. I am sure we'll get to the bottom of this with Carla."

Sam nodded his agreement and expanded on Ben's concluding remark by saying, "Well, I just want to reassure you that I am not selling pipe dreams. I'm doing my best to involve Carla's team as much as possible."

"I trust you, Sam," answered Benjamin.

They went on to discuss Sam's impressions on the sales pipeline. It was satisfactorily brimming with opportunities. His biggest concern, however, was related to prospects who did not follow up after a demonstration or proposal. Sometimes, they were just slow to reach a consensus. Other times, they had decided not to pursue a partnership with Vokeso but would not, for unknown reasons, communicate this information. They literally went silent, ignoring calls and emails, like a diving stealth submarine. This was infuriating and disrespectful to Sam, and he was very vocal about it.

All in all, things were generally going well, and Sam was optimistic they would be closing new deals soon. Benjamin ended the meeting on a positive note for Sam, stating that the team was actively pursuing their training on new technologies and other Microsoft solutions, further fleshing out their portfolio of services and providing Sam with more cross-selling opportunities.

Au Revoir

On the last day of their vacation, Ben and Beth invited Guy and Linda to eat at Mark's Place. Located in the Carrefour Market SXM in Philipsurg, Mark's Place didn't look like much from the outside, but it offered great food: Caribbean as well as American cuisines and generous portions at a good price.

They all drove to the airport, and the group promised one another that they would get together once home. Guy even asked Benjamin if he might call upon his services if needed, to which Ben agreed wholeheartedly. Hugs were exchanged, and then Guy and Linda headed off to catch their flight back to Montreal.[1]

---

[1] This story happened in French Canadian but has been translated to English to spare your sanity.

SECTION 2

SELECTING THE RIGHT TOOL

THE BASICS

Champions are brilliant at the basics.

—John Wooden

> **Key Takeaway: ERP and CRM systems are integrated software systems that help you structure and manage your business!**

One of the key benefits of integrated management systems remains to be the centralization of data. Despite the modular design of such systems, having the information reside in one central database favors the elimination of redundancy, the streamlining of business processes, as well as the quality of said information.

You may be currently going through your corporate life without a bona fide management system. This typically means that you are relying on some accounting package and spreadsheets—many spreadsheets. God only knows where they all live and how they are being maintained. This yarn mix may also include some other applications and databases. A nice spaghetti plate indeed!

Have you ever been in a meeting where two participants argue about numbers that should be the same but, coming from different sources, are not? Have you ever heard of or witnessed people entering data they obtained from one application into another software? Do you only know what you have in stock once a year after a physical count is performed? What if someone just left the company with some knowledge that is nowhere else but in their noggin? Beautiful chaos, if you dig this sort of thing. For most managers and business owners though, this is a living hell...even if *you* are the entrepreneur and the knowledge is in *your* head.

Now, if you recognize these patterns in your business, be concerned, but not worried. We see this all the time. It is a typical situation, which warrants shopping for an ERP. You most likely have outgrown your current accounting solution. Alexis Leon writes in his book *ERP Demystified*, "Having an ERP system is not a luxury but a necessity. It is a must for survival in this competitive world."

Forget the Industrial Age. We now live in the Innovation Age, and the digitization of the world is well underway. Your business needs an ERP system as much as you need to eat well and exercise, the planet needs rainforests, or a championship team needs a top quarterback. *(Perhaps as much as you need a bottle of Tylenol? Not so soon, I hope!)*

Most management systems today become more and more versatile as technology advances further and further at a faster and faster pace. We are literally entering the *Star Trek* age. All right. I concede the point that we are still far from warp speed and the replicator, but the tricorder is almost a reality, and reading tablets are here.

Let us get started by briefly clarifying some concepts.

ERP

An *enterprise resource planning* system is software that helps a company manage and integrate its most important business operations. It will typically include planning, manufacturing, purchasing, inventory, sales, finances, and human resources.

It is often associated with manufacturing companies since it was first introduced to the market quite many years ago as MRP—*materials requirement planning*. Engineer Joseph Orlicky developed MRP in 1964 after studying the Toyota production system. MRP systems were originally focused on handling complex procurement requirements. Throughout their evolution, they included more and more functions until they became the technologically versatile and functionally deep solutions we know today. Today's ERP systems can be used by almost any organization, regardless of size or industry.

ERP applications are typically categorized based on the depth of their functionality and their price tag.

- Tier 1 software packages are the big players: SAP S/4HANA, Oracle, and Microsoft Dynamics Finance & Operations (formerly AX). These solutions are aimed at very large organizations, often multinationals that require important processing capabilities and must handle very large volumes of data.
- Tier 2 ERP systems are more numerous and typically designed for small and medium-sized businesses. Examples are Microsoft Dynamics Business Central, Ross ERP, NetSuite, and Epicor. These systems still offer a good depth of functionality and typically provide some customization capabilities, but at a lower cost. *(The entire SMB world should run Business Central! But I digress. Again. Like the squirrel suffering from ADD in the DreamWorks animation movie* Over the Hedge.*)*
- Finally, tier 3 software is usually less expensive and aimed at smaller companies or perhaps companies who are entering the ERP world for the first time. Microsoft Dynamics GP, QuickBooks, Infor, and Sage 300 come to mind, among many others.

This categorization can become blurry as applications evolve and include more and more of both functional and technical features. You will sometimes find solutions coming from seemingly different tiers competing with one another in certain circumstances.

Cloud

Cloud solutions are growing in popularity as organizations do not want to worry about infrastructure anymore. Interestingly enough, gaming companies were among the first to use the cloud effectively, and their millions of customers were early adopters of this new business model. You can now play games in environments open to all, listen to music without having to store it on your device, and use an ERP system without having to install it on your corporate server.

Cloud solutions can be rolled out in various ways. *Software as a service* (SaaS) applications are offered via subscription. Companies typically pay a monthly fee, by user, to access their software and its features. *Microsoft365*™ is a good SaaS example. NetSuite and Business Central are also offered as SaaS solutions.

In a cloud environment, there often exists a distinction between the applications and the operating system. Even if the operating system is in the cloud, it may be possible to own the ERP system and applications running on your cloud server: this is often referred to as a hybrid cloud. In such a case, only the infrastructure portion of the software is leased while the application licenses are purchased. In a situation like this, you could purchase your Business Central Named User Licenses but have this ERP run on Azure servers in the cloud.

Finally, a cloud environment can be private or public. A *public cloud* is shared by many organizations while maintaining data privacy. In a public cloud, all customers use the same software solutions. A *private cloud* delivers the same advantages as a public cloud, but it is dedicated to a single organization. This approach is often preferred when an organization must address very specific requirements, often related to security or performance concerns.

CRM

The sales and marketing business functions are often handled by *customer relationship management* solutions. CRM software focuses on the marketing and sales cycles and, if not embedded within an ERP system, can complement its functionality through integration. *(You cannot survive in our industry without a profound love for acronyms...as in the military.)*

These solutions will help streamline your sales processes, centralize client information, enable responsive customer service, and provide management and analysis tools such as dashboards and reports.

Just like ERP systems improve and grow their footprint, so do CRM applications. It is not unusual now to find that their scope is enlarged by new offerings such as marketing automation, service management, or customer service features. Microsoft Dynamics 365 Customer Engagement offers five modules: Sales, Marketing, Customer Service, Field Service (*what I call the Maytag™ repairmen module*), and Project Service.

Other CRM applications include Salesforce, Zoho CRM, HubSpot CRM, SugarCRM, etc. Just like ERP systems, CRM software addresses the needs of different company sizes and profiles, so mileage will vary.

HCM

Human capital management applications are often separate solutions or modules specializing in human resources functionality. They provide organizations with the necessary tools to support various operations in their HR department. As employees are now valued as assets, new management approaches need to be translated into HCM features to meet the requirements of companies. Workforce planning, recruitment, talent management, and 360-degree evaluations are examples of features that help support today's human resources departments.

Payroll processing can sometimes be included in HCM solutions. You can also find payroll processing bundled into some ERP systems. As payroll processing is very regional, payroll solutions can often be found as standalone solutions. Some vendors compete with payroll solutions by offering payroll processing services.

LIMS

Laboratory information management systems provide functionalities that help enterprises manage their laboratories. Sometimes used in manufacturing companies, these particular applications often support quality assurance and quality control departments. Depending on the depth of the solution, their features can sometimes intersect and interact with those of an ERP system.

MES

ERP systems often include functionality to support manufacturing operations. You could say that many ERP solutions include a *manufacturing execution system*. According to Wikipedia, an MES monitors, tracks, documents, and controls the process of manufacturing goods from raw materials to finished products. If you acquire a separate MES solution, you will most likely need to pair it with an accounting package. Your MES better be really good, if not extraordinary, to justify discarding the functionality offered by your ERP platform.

Mobility

In today's shrinking world, characterized by a global market, company resources and partners are often distributed around the globe. Mobility and cloud become strategic elements of modern-day management systems. Mobility allows access to your management system from almost anywhere—anywhere you can use a phone or tablet that is. *(Indeed, your freedom is forfeited. You carry your electronic leash with you anywhere you go, and it now comes with one of the most expensive software on earth!)*

Emerging 5G networks will further emphasize this trend by improving connectivity among various devices, supporting Industry 4.0, and enabling the nomad workers of the world, especially after COVID-19 has demonstrated the feasibility of the remote worker model.

Like many others, I have been working remotely for years, and as mentalities change, it becomes even easier. I have also worked while out of the country, thanks to tools like Teams and Zoom. *(Okay, I have not yet tried to remote work on top of Mount Everest, but that's just because I do not have satellite communication and am too lazy to climb up there.)*

SCM

Supply chain management focuses on the flow of goods from, to, and within the organization. Movement and storage of raw materials, work-in-process inventory, and finished goods are tracked throughout the manufacturing or distribution cycle, from supplier to customer. Most ERP systems now include an SCM module or functionality that supports purchasing, planning, and logistics.

WMS

Warehouse management systems can either be a component or an extension of ERP systems. Where ERP systems always include basic inventory control transactions, WMS systems take it a few steps further, with streamlined processes supporting high transactional volumes by using barcoding functionality and automation. WMS allows you to go paperless. High-end systems may include tracking and routing technologies such as *radio frequency identification* (RFID) or even voice recognition.

WMS software is often available as a module or even as a separate application. Not all companies have a need for this level of sophistication or are ready for it yet. If you are implementing

ERP for the first time, you may want to walk before you run, and enabling WMS could be a later deployment phase.

❧ ❧ ❧

Now that you have been thoroughly hammered with acronyms, you need to know that we have only skimmed the frothy surface. Hopefully, the few icy peaks that have now been rendered visible to you will be enough to get you through this incredibly awesome book in one great read. Do not think too much about the hidden portions of proverbial icebergs for now. We will try to go around them before they sink your ship.

As you meticulously study this delectable book to absorb all its revealed secrets, should you encounter an expression or new acronym you do not understand or that is not explained to your satisfaction, I recommend you do what the industry experts do: google it! *(Google, like engineers, knows everything.)*

CAUSES FOR CHANGE

Change is inevitable. progress is optional.

—Tony Robbins

> **Key Takeaway: We say change is good, but when it relates to your business applications, it is usually forced upon you. Be aware of the ramifications so you can deal with the challenge appropriately.**

For many, navigating the ERP landscape feels like walking through a minefield without a metal detector, scaling a precipice without a climbing rope, or even walking around with a rock in your shoe— infuriating. To you, it may be a dangerous world populated with nightmarish salespeople, frightening computer geeks, and even worse, financial rifts that can materialize anywhere, anytime, to suck all your hard-earned cash into another dimension. Have I vividly communicated the required level of empathy to draw you in? I sure hope so! Ghostbusters can't help you here.

The ERP industry can be frustratingly complicated. Implementing a new management system is usually a very delicate and risky operation. As complex and scary as it may be, just like a heart transplant, it is usually necessary for the individual requiring it.

If you are contemplating an ERP project, then you may be facing one of a few realities that are usually conducive to such an endeavor. Let us explore some of them.

Compliance

Compliance can often be a strong motivator forcing companies to consider buying an ERP system. These regulatory requirements may be the result of a new law, a failed audit, an entry into a new market, or a significant growth revealing your existing systems' inability to cope with important regulations. Either way, rules imposed by governments and their institutions can be critical. Just think about The Sarbanes-Oxley Act of 2002, which has forced companies and their systems to increase their level of task segregation, security, and controls. Another example is the Federal Food, Drug, and Cosmetics Act enforced by the US Food and Drug Administration, which imposes *good manufacturing practices*. GMPs rely on key functionality, like lot traceability and quality control. Most ERP systems can support or facilitate compliance by promoting and adhering to operational best practices.

External Pressures

Your competition may be twisting your arm. As you notice them edging you on price or gaining ground in the market, you may conclude after proper analysis that your organization needs to tweak its performance. Improving efficiency can help you cut costs or become nimbler. Perhaps you need to instill robustness into your operations, allowing you to tap new markets. This evolution can often be fueled by deploying a better management system; sometimes it even becomes imperative.

Evolution

Your business is growing. You are developing new products, making acquisitions, and generally moving in the right direction. Yet that success comes at a price: you feel your control ebbing. New requirements crop up. It becomes harder and harder for your current business systems to keep pace with your transforming organization. It might therefore be time to mitigate the use of Excel and your cheap accounting system and invest in an integrated solution that will improve your business practices.

❧ ❧ ❧

This last example is quite positive, but one way or another, you will typically be pushed and coerced toward a system change by forces out of your control. This can mold your relationship with your ERP system, just like your relationship with money can often be influenced by various events in your life. No one should claim that your ERP project will be easy, but keep in mind that it is certainly necessary and worth your full attention as a strategic business project.

The main goal of an ERP implementation is to improve the efficiency of the company by automating processes, streamlining workflows, reducing costs, and increasing productivity. Below are six benefits of implementing an ERP:

1. **Centralized data**
    Having your data stored in one system creates a single source of truth. This supports data accuracy and continued improvements in decision-making processes and builds trust in your data.
2. **Real-time information**
    Your ERP system should support all your transactions in real time, allowing you to make informed decisions. Real-time information can be the foundation of business intelligence. Key performance indicators can provide instant visibility into problems and eliminate best guesses.
3. **Best practices**
    ERP systems are built and configured with best practices in mind. Deploying an ERP will help standardize your processes and should also mitigate exception handling. Companies that operate without an ERP system often rely on convoluted and complex processes that have devolved out of control over time.
4. **Operational efficiency**
    ERP solutions can improve the efficiency of your operations across your various departments. Better planning can help reduce production downtime, lower stock levels, and shorten lead times. Automation can improve data accuracy

while significantly accelerating various transactions. Centralized data and robust processes can speed up month-end closing.

5. **Controlled costs**

   Controlling costs is often a blind spot for companies as the data may not be accurate and available in real time. All the reasons mentioned above have an impact on controlling and reducing costs. Having the ability to measure something gives you the ability to improve it.

6. **Client satisfaction**

   Finally, there should be a strong correlation between the operational benefits provided by your ERP software and customer satisfaction. Your customers are at the end of your supply chain, and any improvement within the chain should ultimately benefit them with better pricing, improved visibility, better quality products, quicker lead times, etc.

Case Study

My very first customer decided, back in 1998, to implement an ERP system to support their operations. We were in the midst of the Y2K scramble, and until then, they had been using a local solution developed by a micro company that had eventually gone bust. They were vulnerable. They chose a tier 2 solution now called Ross ERP. This software is specifically built for process manufacturing companies.

They went live in 1999 with two manufacturing plants. They deployed a solution that supported multiple currencies and multiple companies, specifically sustained their business processes, and could scale with the business. They have continued investing in their ERP over the years and performed various acquisitions, and they are now number one in their industry.

Self-preservation and survival were their original moti-vators, but a good toolbox gave them the leverage they needed to grow. (Of course, they could count on us—their secret weapon!)

BUSINESS CASE

Document your dreams. Sketch that shape you saw.
Write those lyrics before they fade out.
—Michael Bassey Johnson

Key Takeaway: Once you realize change is inevitable and you are at the threshold, document your situation to quantify the impact of that change on your business.

The business case is a useful decision-making tool that can be applied to your ERP project in various ways. Even if it seems costly and tedious at first, the benefits can be great. Think about it. If you are a parent, you've been in this situation. Every day of our lives as parents, our kids present us with all these nice business cases they passionately develop. They need this or must have that. Absolutely should go there. Yesterday.

Why do they work so hard? To obtain what they so desperately require to function in this pitiless, harsh world. They always get approval from the board of directors, don't they? *(Yup. I am a parent, three times over that I am aware of, and I survived thus far! I am only kidding. I know it's not more than three. Could it be less?)*

It is good practice to build a business case to document the key motivators justifying the acquisition of a new ERP system and the benefits it should bring the organization. Depending on the size of your business and its decision structure, creating a business case for major projects may already be common practice. If not, it may be the right time to seriously consider it.

Your internal business case may be used as a valuable analysis report for your management team, facilitating the commitment process and organization of the necessary funding. Consultants can also help you put this document together.

In French, we use the expression *cahier des charges*. I like that term. Although the common English translation is "specifications," I would freely translate *cahier des charges* to something like "a notebook of prices." In French, *charge* has multiple meanings. It can also represent a responsibility or commitment. How about "a notebook of engagements"?

A business case can also be developed by your vendor's solution sales team to demonstrate the value of implementing their application in your organization. The case should highlight the benefits of the solution by presenting the estimated return on investment (ROI) and total cost of ownership (TCO).

If various sales teams are required to contribute a business case for you, they will need your help in creating their deliverable. Your own business case can come in handy and provide valuable and homogenous information to all parties involved.

External business cases from your suppliers will help you compare the various solutions presented to you during the proposal stage of your project.

Throughout this process, the focus is usually on the financial costs and measurable benefits, but I would be remiss not to mention other returns that often represent significant pieces of the puzzle: efficiencies gained, troop motivation, market competitiveness, and so on.

A sample document can be found here: www.erphelp.co/down-loadables.

Case Study

Bryan had been trying for years to obtain a reasonable budget from the board so he would be able to replace their old ERP system. This endeavor never seemed to get enough visibility and interest to become a priority. After all, most users had never known anything else and seemed content with their existing legacy system.

Bryan knew, however, that their system was outdated. The technology was long in the tooth, and it was hard to find related help on the market. The application had stopped evolving, and people were compensating with spreadsheets and manual remedies. The business was vulnerable and could really benefit from modernizing its operations. After all, there were some great solutions out there.

What won the day in the end was Bryan's decision to in-vest some time and money in a formal business case. The analysis performed by an outside firm revealed an inter-esting financial return on investment but also demonstrat-ed how a new application would help the organization achieve its strategic growth plan. The business case was judiciously aligned with the company's five-year strate-gic plan and within that context made all the sense in the world. (Sorry, I don't have anything funny to add. This is so amazing, I'm at a loss for words.)

REQUIREMENTS AND ROAD MAP

Knowing ~~yourself~~ **your business** and what it needs
is the beginning of all wisdom.

—Sylvain, after Aristotle

> **Key Takeaway: Determine what your business requires and where you want to take it before you commit to buying an ERP.**

It may seem useless or superfluous to promote knowledge of your business, but surveys have shown that an inadequate definition of functional requirements accounts for nearly 60 percent of ERP implementation failures. A thorough identification of your business needs is mandatory to select the appropriate system for your business and obtain the benefits your company deserves.

Why would such a process be cause for failure when, at first glance, it should prove simple enough to gather information about your operations? I will really go out on a limb here and blame your own people!

(Oh, hey, take a break before throwing ripe tomatoes!)

Here is the rationale behind my statement. Keep in mind that the most important component of any business system—and also, arguably, its most fragile—is its people. Therefore, it stands to reason that they would be an integral part of the solution or, perhaps, the problem.

The first aspect of a functional-requirements-gathering exercise consists of documenting the business. It is not uncommon for small and medium-sized businesses to grow without taking time to document their processes and procedures. In such a situation, your people are often keepers of the knowledge. You may find some documentation here and there, but more often than not, the information is in their heads...and whatever is in someone's head can be hard to extract. *(This reminds me of an anecdote involving my girlfriend and telepathy. Well, maybe I should not go there.)*

I recommend taking time and investing in the documentation of your business processes and procedures. They may change when you implement your solution, but at least you will have a solid foundation to work with. We will further discuss business process documentation in a later chapter.

Ultimately, you want to identify what features you will require in your new ERP system. Listing requirements based on how you currently operate is a good start. Do you need lot traceability, multicurrency processing, or average costing?

It should be noted that you will also be looking for opportunities to improve your operations, and it would therefore be appropriate to venture forth looking for weaknesses in your various departments. Your primary motivation is to get better. Be sensitive to how this may be perceived by your employees as it can represent an underlying issue that must be tackled.

As you take a hard look at your business processes and try to be as honest as possible about areas of inefficiency, you are in some ways criticizing how those people perform their jobs today. You are challenging business systems your employees may have helped structure, promote, and support in the past; this can quickly put them on the defensive. Moreover, most people have a hard time dealing with change. This is why change management, which we will discuss in future chapters, is so important.

You ultimately want to retrieve the knowledge your people possess but also get them openly involved in the improvement of operations. This is how they can be part of the solution, not the problem.

Another aspect of a well-rounded requirements analysis that should not be neglected consists of fleshing out a future operational and functional road map for your organization. Should you automate bank reconciliations? Rely on optical character recognition to scan purchase invoices? Project cash flow levels using artificial intelligence? Deploy visual planning in your manufacturing division or perhaps integrate your ERP system with your machines using the Internet of Things?

Learning about your current weaknesses and documenting them goes hand in hand with ideating an improved reality for your business. Your leadership is thus vital if you wish to rally your troops around this mission-critical yet disturbing corporate goal. After all, this important step will help benchmark the success of your implementation and define your true return on investment.

Case Study

I have had the experience of working with customers who did not sufficiently think things through before committing to an ERP implementation. Not having clear requirements to work with hindered the establishment of a well-defined scope and explicit objectives. It made us vulnerable to scope creep.

There was much back and forth going on between users, management, and the project team to determine what functionality should be implemented. It also opened the door to multiple demands for customizations. These tergiversations slowed the project down and caused budget overruns and a ton of frustration. This can be exacerbated when the deployment involves important functional gaps or complex integrations with other systems.

In all instances, we still managed to go live, but the twisting paths that were taken could have been much straighter.

REQUEST FOR INFORMATION

As a general rule, the most successful man in life is
the man who has the best information.

—Benjamin Disraeli

**Key Takeaway: An RFI can help you find out what
you do not know but should know.**

A *request for information* is occasionally used by some
organizations, such as governmental institutions or companies
operating under unusual circumstances, to collect information
about suppliers and their solutions. The purpose of this exercise is
to find vendors that can potentially participate in a future bidding
process or perhaps explore the market to discover what solutions
are available to the company.

Think of this RFI process as someone walking into a shoe store and
trying on a dozen pairs without buying any, just to see which one
might look good. Coming out of there, the shopper will have a very
good understanding of what kind of shoe might be appropriate.
The salesperson, however, will certainly hope the shopper doesn't
go online to make a purchase and eventually returns to buy one!

It's not all bad though. RFI could mean *request for interest* as those
vendors who participate know what they are getting into and most
likely hope to participate in the follow-up bidding process. An RFI
is structured and organized to promote comparisons between
submissions and should be less involved than a full-fledged
request for proposal, which we will discuss in the next chapter.

If you intend to go through with this activity, you might want to consider the scope of your project against the benefits of such an endeavor. It could represent a significant amount of work for both the organization and the participating suppliers. As such, the forms and templates you use should be aligned with the size of your project.

As an example, an RFI published a few years ago by a small- and medium-sized company was one simple spreadsheet with about a dozen questions oriented toward finding a solution that could potentially meet their industry requirements.

Another one sent out by a university included a fourteen-page corporate informational PDF, an open questionnaire of about one hundred questions, and a request to perform a demo. *(It came from a university, so where is the surprise here? They like shoveling clouds, don't they?)*

Guess which one the vendors would prefer to fill in? Eventually, someone on your staff will also have the responsibility of analyzing all these forms once they are returned to you completed.

Sample documents can be found here: www.erphelp.co/down-loadables.

Case Study

This telecommunications company, not a big player, was curious to know if there were any affordable SMB solutions in the market specifically geared toward their sector.

They sent out a brief request for information questionnaire to as many solution vendors as they could find. The questionnaire was brief but to the point. It was quick and easy to fill out and would obviously be returned if anyone had a solution that fit the high-level requirements depicted in the form. Vendors who returned it would be invited to participate in the RFP process once a second look at them revealed them as a true contender.

This process was driven by an ERP selection consultant I know and, under the circumstances, was well executed. To me, it remains one of the best RFIs I have seen.

REQUEST FOR PROPOSAL

~~Information~~ **An RFP** is only useful when it can be understood.

—Sylvain, after Muriel Cooper

> **Key Takeaway: The RFP can be a good tool to evaluate software solutions, but it requires discipline: be careful how you use it.**

The *request for proposal* is an invitation to vendors to bid on a project. This structured process is usually quite deliberate and involved. Organizations will generally get the help of an outside consultant or consulting firm specializing in such demanding exercises.

The request for proposal is a formal process with specific requirements and templates, trading information about the company for information about the vendor and his solution.

The *request for quote* (RFQ) should not be confused with the RFP. The RFQ is usually just asking for a price and is therefore a much simpler process.

The RFP is based on the principle that the winning bidder should be selected impartially based on predefined criteria important to the organization and its operations. Features of the solution are thoroughly evaluated, as is the vendor's reputation and ability to deliver.

To successfully accomplish this analytical selection, the vendors will be provided with valuable information about the company's history, current situation, and future objectives. Vendors will also be required to provide information about themselves and complete a lengthy and detailed functional requirements questionnaire, usually an Excel spreadsheet. Responses will typically involve some kind of numerical value helping to quantify the ability of the software to meet the requirements. *(On occasion, emphasis seems to be placed on the "anal" part of "analysis." I suppose someone has to justify their fee.)*

Below is an example of typical responses to a question on capability that would be about a feature or functionality:

7. Supported in the current release of the software
6. Supported in a future release available in the next zero to six months
5. Supported by a third-party add-on product
4. Supported via a workaround
3. Supported with a minor software modification
2. Supported in a future release available in the next seven to twelve months
1. Supported with a major software modification

Each question will also be weighed based on its importance to the customer:

4. Critical priority
3. Very high priority
2. Medium priority
1. Low priority

Once all RFP documents have been gathered—and it is not uncommon to have a dozen vendors involved—a preselection is conducted where two or three suppliers will be retained to advance to the next step in the selection process. We will discuss these steps in upcoming chapters.

Caveat Emptor

Chapter 3 emphasized the importance of defining your requirements before venturing forth into the selection process. An RFP
is the ultimate requirements-gathering machine. *Ad nauseam.*
Though one may think that such a process guarantees the impartial selection of the best vendor and software for the job...that is not
always the case.

Despite all these Cartesian manipulations, keep in mind that you
have people filling in the questionnaires, people supervising the
process, and people getting involved in the final decision. As
rational as you may imagine the RFP purchasing process to be,
in the end, it remains an emotional decision, as are all buying
decisions.

I do not make these things up; neuroscience does. Nobel laureate
Herbert A. Simon believes impartial economic decision-making to
be out of reach and always "tainted" by emotional and nonrational
considerations. *(I would agree with him. After all, he won a Nobel
Prize, did he not?)*

Here are some examples of the human factor disrupting a purely
analytical methodology:

- The selection consultant may be biased toward a certain
  vendor.
- The selection committee may be biased against a given
  solution based on an article read online recently.
- Since the requirements were gathered by department,
  some questions were duplicated.
- The vendor attempted to respond to the questionnaire as
  factually as he could, but ultimately, he wants to make the
  first cut, so...

- The vendor attempted to respond to the questionnaire as factually as possible, but he was skewed by his knowledge of his system and his experience.
- The vendor attempted to respond to the questionnaire as factually as possible, but he misunderstood a few questions.

I would also point out that you can sometimes see a difference when consultants supporting a selection process have not implemented ERP before. It becomes more theoretical.

So long as everyone involved remembers that an RFP process is not infallible, it can prove to be a useful tool to help you through a complicated selection process. Chances are the two or three finalists will be very close to one another. The final decision will most likely be greatly influenced by intangible factors such as confidence, good vibes from the project team, etc.

Sample documents can be found here: www.erphelp.co/down-loadables.

Case Study

This topic is rich in real-life examples. I once participated in this tedious, detailed, meticulous, lengthy, thorough request for proposal. The questionnaire had thousands of questions supported by various documents and more forms to fill in, all for a tier 2 selection process and a prospect that had one information system professional on its roster. We are not talking about Pratt & Whitney Canada here but a regular medium-sized company. This whole adventure must have cost them a fortune. Did I mention that the process included two demonstrations before we were eliminated? This means that the vendor who was chosen probably had to demo three times.

To this day, I wonder if they ended up making the right decision. The prospect had been through a nightmarish experience with customizations in the past, and they were very biased against it—and understandably so. That being said, our solution was a good fit despite involving some customizations. We also believed other solutions also had gaps, but less flexibility to handle them.

We'll probably never know, but at the of the day, it seemed to me that the emotional baggage tied to their previous experience might have tainted their intended rational and methodical selection process. (Of course, I am in no way emotionally biased in thinking the solution we offered was the best.)

DISCOVERY

The greatest obstacle to discovery is not
ignorance—it is the illusion of knowledge.
—Daniel J. Boorstin

Key Takeaway: You should include a presales discovery in your selection process, and you should use it to your advantage.

A discovery is a very valuable tool for vendors when trying to assess the requirements of a prospective customer. Someone from the presales group would typically visit your organization and meet with you and your people. The primary objective is to achieve a significant understanding of your operations, your current challenges, and your future direction. A plant tour is usually included, if applicable. This is almost mandatory if a specifications document (*notebook of prices*) was not produced.

A properly conducted discovery will provide additional and interesting insight into your organization that cannot be achieved with a document included in a request for proposal. Very often, formal RFP processes will exclude a discovery because of time constraints or an attempt to be fair to all vendors. An RFP without a discovery serves as a great example of imparting your participating vendors with the illusion of knowledge. Meeting face-to-face with people and physically visiting the premises is a greatly enhanced experience, far more worthwhile than reading and interpreting a document; reading someone's profile on a dating site can be very informative, but it does not compare with meeting them in person.

Another benefit of discoveries is the opportunity it provides you to evaluate the vendors' ability to understand what you do and what you face. It will also provide impressions into the vendor's culture and overall approach: you can inquire about their vision for your organization and get a feel for the intangibles they can bring to the table.

To your supplier, a discovery is akin to a designer visiting the home she will redesign versus studying it from a plan; the level of inspiration is not comparable. To you, it is an opportunity to see your designer's twinkling eyes as she begins to envision the true potential of your renovated home.

Having said all that, I have noticed a change in recent years. The landscape is different from when I wrote the first edition of this book. Smaller organizations can now access tier 2 functionality via SaaS ERP solutions. Much information is available on the internet, and sometimes, trial environments can even be configured and experienced by prospective customers. The functionality is being democratized.

Moreover, remote work has become the norm following COVID. For all these reasons, most discoveries I have conducted in recent years have been shorter and virtual. On occasion, my client already knows what they want. Other times, their processes seem simple enough.

I would presently recommend an on-site discovery if your documentation is lacking or if your operations are complex, especially in a distribution or manufacturing environment.

Case Study

I once briefly argued with a prospect's project sponsor that I should visit them first to perform a discovery before providing a demo of the application. Since customers (and prospects) are always right (and maybe I am too much of a yes-man), I agreed to follow his lead and showed up to demo my software. With five or six people around the table, it didn't take long before I started fielding questions about functionality they expected to see but I could not show.

We concluded that the generic demonstration I was about to perform was not appropriate and that they needed to see more specific features. Moreover, there were other vendors out there who seemed more specialized in the apparel industry than we were.

I would have been able to provide the same counsel had we first gone through a discovery. That approach, however, would have cost less time on both sides and involved fewer people.

DEMONSTRATIONS

The world needs demonstration more than it needs
teaching.

—Wallace D. Wattles

**Key Takeaway: Software demonstrations are key
when selecting ERP...provided they truly address
your business concerns.**

As stated in the previous chapter, the discovery is important for
your vendor to understand your current situation. The goal behind
the discovery is to find out what troubles your organization is
currently experiencing and how best to address these issues with
a new software solution. The true objective, however, is to gather
enough evidence to build an effective and pertinent software
demonstration.

The demonstration, if well executed, should address your
organizational concerns and illustrate how your new ERP will
improve the situation. It is the demonstrator's mandate to guide you
effectively across a virtual bridge that separates your immediate
and known reality under your legacy system from your future
operational landscape using the new application.

It has been recommended that, as a rule, presales consultants
should not perform live transactions for the audience. This is a rule
that I have personally adopted. Keying in transactions is a very risky
proposal as things can go wrong for various reasons, and once
error messages start popping up, the whole shebang becomes a
very confusing ordeal.

Your people will lose track of the flow once the consultant jumps left and right to fix the problem. Moreover, even when things go smoothly, watching someone populate fields on the screen is far from exciting. *(Anyone facing more than ten minutes of live data entry projected on the wall would rather watch Congress debate live on C-SPAN television.)*

The presenter's primary job is to tell a story. This would be an often-heard expression in the presales guild—assuming there was such a guild. Telling a story is creating a believable visualization of what the new system will be able to accomplish for the viewers: showing the system becomes more important than using it; describing the future is more important than showcasing the features. Your employees gathered in the meeting room must be inspired to see and imagine how the new system will help their day-to-day lives by solving their problems, without creating new ones.

Considering the importance of the demonstration and the number of people it will usually mobilize, it is vital for the vendor to be given enough time and information to create the best possible event. Can you imagine a movie without the props, sets, and costumes? Chewbacca without the fur probably would not sell too many figurines! How believable is Jack teaching Rose to fly in front of the *Titanic*, without the computer-generated background?

Demo Scripts

When preparing for the demo, the presales consultant will generate a script that will typically illustrate various business processes that are important to your organization. The script is obviously dependent upon the software being shown and the business requirements of the prospective customer. The value of the script can be increased with proprietary data that your organization can provide to make the demo more realistic.

Whenever you decide to influence the demo by imposing your own scripts, it should be remembered that your vision of how the application will perform is not yet clear, even if your future road map is properly defined. As such, it is not unusual for the demo to diverge from your intended flow as the consultant attempts to adapt your script to his application's functional flow. Nonetheless, when all is said and done, all required transactions, operations, and processes should have been properly covered.

Evaluation

If you hire a consultant to help you select the proper ERP, you will most likely be provided with an evaluation grid based on your requirements. This grid will help you score the solution and vendor based on various predefined and often-weighted criteria. When evaluating a demonstration, it is important to remember that you are not evaluating the presales consultant's performance. He may not be the best speaker—perhaps he is boring even—but the focus should be on the solution, not the quality of the show. *(Lucky for you, if you ever attend one of my demos, we have a ton of fun. You've already gotten a glimpse of my stellar humor.)*

Moreover, chances are that the presales consultant will not be implementing your solution. Even though we like working with knowledgeable people, you ultimately want the implementation team to be more knowledgeable than your presales consultant. *(I used to be a consultant, and I was clearly smarter back then. Maybe it doesn't have anything to do with selling and more with growing old?)*

On occasion, implementation consultants will accompany the presales consultant to support him or perhaps present some topics.

The final demonstration is the pivotal event. It is usually after the final demo that your selection committee has enough information to reach a tipping point and make the call.

Case Study

A survey conducted by Panorama Consulting Solutions in 2016 revealed that only 4 percent of responders claimed that their ERP purchase was driven by the best demonstration. This would seem to indicate that other factors, such as Best Functional Fit at 46 percent, play a more important role in the selection process. When you stop to consider the other possible answers the survey provided: Best Value for Money (25 percent), Commonly Used in our Industry (13 percent), and Other (10 percent), you begin to understand why Best Demonstration gathered such limited support.

I would argue that the offered answers probably were mutually exclusive, and they should not have been. I can hardly imagine a company buying an ERP package because the functional fit looked great in the requirements questionnaire, completely ignoring the demo. It seems to me someone could buy an ERP because it offered the best functional fit for the budgeted money and that the demo proved it. You see my point?

GAP ANALYSIS

Price is what you pay. Value is what you get.

—Warren Buffet

Key Takeaway: The fit-gap analysis focuses on the areas of the system that do not meet business requirements. It identifies customizations and their cost.

Even though the functional coverage of modern ERP systems continues to improve, it is not atypical to find functional gaps when evaluating an ERP solution...unless you can find one specifically tailored to your industry. Even then, it may not be a one-hundred-percent fit: whether your business needs a specific report or a fully customized feature, you may find yourself with gaps to address.

Deployment methodologies account for this analysis, and it is thus normally performed during the design phase. The deliverable obtained is a document that describes, in simple business terms, how the application will be modified to meet your business requirements and an estimate of what the cost of these adaptations should be.

This is where the rubber meets the pavement: this gap analysis is what makes your project different from other projects. This is the space that you truly own as an organization. This is often where your software vendor will make a significant difference in the implementation considering the risk customizations represent. If your ERP implementation was a sailboat, then your fit-gap analysis would be your anchor. You really want to make sure your ship will not drift!

The fit-gap analysis is often written during the design phase as users and consultants test the application and find areas of improvement. Each customization presented in the document needs to be reviewed by the steering committee and accepted, rejected, or postponed.

Implementing an ERP system is an iterative process, going from the general to the specific. *(This expression I learned many years ago in university, and I like to use it as often as I can to show how smart I am. I also like using the word* propensity—*big word, that one.)*

It is not unusual to find functional gaps during the presales cycle. The requirements questionnaire and the demonstrations often reveal such functional limitations.

Considering the importance of this task and the anticipated scope of the gaps, you could mandate your selected vendor to write a fit-gap analysis even before the deal is signed. Why wait until someone gets hurt before repairing the handrail?

You could make this a prerequisite of the final decision. You will obviously have to spend money at this point, but this minor investment, in comparison to the cost of choosing the wrong solution or the wrong vendor, should be well worth it, especially if your business requirements are complex and unique. The fit-gap analysis can thus become a software selection tool.

A sample fit-gap analysis document can be found here: www.erphelp.co/downloadables.

Case Study

Many years ago, one of my customers experienced great difficulty deploying the manufacturing modules of his ERP system. Over time, they had dealt with different partner vendors who had customized their applications without properly documenting their work. We concluded that a re-implementation was more appropriate than a version upgrade. We also took the time to perform an initial gap analysis. That was very beneficial as the project was ultimately delivered on time and under budget. The fit-gap analysis allowed us to define a realistic budget and plan the project accordingly.

More recently, a prospective customer asked us to perform a fit-gap analysis before committing to the project. We knew during presales there would be gaps, but further analysis revealed an unexpected twist as the data model required to support their business processes was much more convoluted. It resulted in a more complex design that would, however, streamline a larger portion of the business than they previously expected.

We saw more benefit to the organization but at a greater cost. With this knowledge, the company decided to look for financing and probably saved us all from much frustration and headaches down the line. Imagine finding this out one-third into the completion of the project!

PROTOTYPING

I have not failed. I've just found ten thousand ways
that won't work.

—Thomas Edison

> **Key Takeaway: a prototype is a rudimentary
> mock-up of an application or, more appropriately,
> a set of business customizations.**

Full-blown prototyping is not often used in ERP software selection
processes, but if you know of a significant, mission-critical, and
very complex functional gap, you might want to consider pushing
the analysis further by designing a working model of what the full
solution would look like.

It can be difficult for some individuals to work from analysis
documents when designing and defining a custom development,
as difficult as it may be for people to visualize their home or
renovation project from a two-dimensional plan. Television shows
about landscaping and renovation have their designers resort to
3D-modeling tools to render their vision and get buy-in from their
clients: a prototype serves the same purpose.

As a board game enthusiast, I am often exposed to such prototypes,
and I have had the privilege of testing a few: they do not look very
good, but still convey the essence of the game. The *metagame*, as
it is called, can be understood. The mechanics can be tested, and
although the experience is not as immersive as the final product
will be, it does allow you to determine if the game is one you will
like or not. *(Another interesting piece of trivia about yours truly: I
am a geek.)*

By building some screens and reports, developers will provide concrete visual cues that can help users imagine how the new module would work, and just as importantly, it will help them think of other requirements they may have inadvertently omitted. The working model that gets built will not include many business rules and validations; the logic behind key functions might also be fake. Again, the purpose is to provide enough visualization to get user acceptance.

This process may seem costly and time-consuming at first, but chances are that it will help save redundant effort later in the project. Less effort is less money spent. Less money spent means fewer headaches and more fun for you. Moreover, the prototype, if successful, is not wasted time but represents the skeleton frame upon which the rest of the solution will be developed.

Case Study

One area where prototypes can be used, albeit on a small scale, is in demonstrations. I often ask my developers to quickly put something together before a software demonstration so I can show my audience that I understand a particular functional gap and how we might be able to address it in the ERP.

This is what I call movie props. They look great from afar, but when you get closer, you realize they're not real buildings but just a painting.

For me, screens and reports are not important. What counts is the data model. Can the tables and fields support the business requirement? If so, screens and reports will not be an issue. Users, however, will be searching for familiarity when they watch a demonstration. They reg-

ularly want to see their own data as it helps them cross that bridge to the future that we discussed in the chapter on demonstrations. A movie prop serves to achieve the same objective.

PROOF OF CONCEPT

But the best demonstration by far is experience, if it
goes not beyond the actual experiment.

—Francis Bacon

> **Key Takeaway: A proof of concept aims to il-
> lustrate the usability of an ERP solution be-
> yond what can be learned from a conventional
> demonstration.**

A proof of concept is common in product development. Although
the line blurs between proof of concept, prototype, and minimal
viable product, these efforts share the same purpose: they
demonstrate the value of an idea. In television, pilots represent
a proof of concept. It is also interesting to note that movies and
television series are now likewise being made based on small
videos produced by individuals who wish to share their ideas. It
is no longer necessary to rely on the classic approach: scripts,
treatments, pitches, and book options.

An ERP proof of concept can be useful when the challenge is
to determine the applicability of the standard solution regarding
specific, often unconventional requirements of your organization.
It is not unusual for the presales consultant to find ways that
functionality meant for a certain business application can be used
to meet other, similar needs.

In cases where these functional requirements are not few and
simple but encompass a large portion of the software solution and
reach a certain level of complexity, it may be appropriate to prepare

a representative sample of data and run transactions through to make sure the concept works.

This is essentially the same approach as piloting the system, which involves performing integrated, process-based testing. It is, however, executed before the software is selected, not during the deployment phase: the proof of concept serves to validate that the system considered for purchase can support the business.

It is my opinion that a prototype will help visualize a customization while the proof of concept will help validate a configuration.

Case Study

One of our customers was wondering if our integrated CRM-ERP solution could be used to fulfill some of their particular business requirements in a given business area. They had to decide between using our product and that of a competitor. They requested a proof of concept to help in their evaluation. We configured our product to meet their requirements and explained how some of the gaps could be addressed.

It is interesting to note that we did not prototype those gaps as decision-makers were still able to anticipate how the solution would work.

Performing the transactions and being able to see how the system handled their operations was very helpful to them. We invested about two weeks in this little project, but it probably saved them a lot more time and money downstream, having been able to make an enlightened call early on.

VERTICALIZATION

To apply general tools to specific problems is to fail.
—Michael Crichton

Key Takeaway: Business systems are evolving to the point where they are now being built for specific industries.

It used to be that you were in a good position whenever you found an ERP system that could meet 80 percent of your business requirements. Almost every project involved a fair number of customizations, increasing deployment time and dollars spent.

In his book *ERP Demystified*, Alexis Leon states, "The organizational culture and the nature of projects will be different from company to company. Thus, two ERP implementations can never be identical."

In the first edition of my book, my spellchecker was telling me *verticalization* is not a word. It clearly is now, and it is an answer to the above statement from Mr. Leon. Solutions have evolved to the point where most applications now offer great functional coverage of all commonly known operations, and it is becoming harder and harder to select the best generic solution.

Software vendors are now looking for niche markets to increase their piece of the pie. By promoting verticalization through their partner channel or by adapting their solutions themselves, they are trying to meet the requirements of specific industries.

The benefit for the vendor or partner is obvious: finding a less-crowded playing field. Less competition means shorter and easier sales cycles, as well as higher margins due to the additional value brought to the table.

The benefit for the customer is finding a solution that is better tailored to their needs. This entails fewer customizations, easier deployments, and a greater return on investment.

As you enter your selection process, you may want to pay close attention and first look for solutions built for your industry. They may not have been there three years ago but could be now! Another option may be to develop a special business relationship with a vendor who is willing to specialize in your industry. A request for information, discussed in a previous chapter, could be a good tool to support your research.

Case Study

Depending on the industry, verticalizing *may not be as hard as it seems. Sometimes, just a few adaptations to add wanted features, such as the 5 percent retainer in the construction industry, and modeling the user experience (UX) to match commonly used functions can be enough.*

In other situations, verticalizing can be time-consuming, expensive, and risky. A local partner is currently investing significant resources in adapting Microsoft D365 Business Central for the undertaker industry. I have heard of companies targeting the automotive, pharmaceutical, and printing industries. And it's tough!

As for us, through a combination of experience, intellectual property, and partner solutions, we have a knack for manufacturing, and half of our customer base is composed of companies in that sector.

FINDING THE RIGHT PARTNER

One can't avoid the storms and calamities of life,
but one can at least find the right partner to face
them with.

—Lisa Kleypas

> **Key Takeaway: Selecting the right partner to work
> with is essential and maybe even more important
> than the solution you purchase.**

Selecting the right application is key, but as ERP solutions mature, you may find that more than one solution you are evaluating can effectively meet your requirements. What then becomes the deciding factor? Correct...the vendor! Hum, maybe not, but please bear with me.

A study conducted by Panorama Consulting shows that "Best Functional Fit" and "Best Value for Money" are the top two reasons for selecting an ERP.

In a world filled with value-added resellers, the "Best Value for Money" is often tied to the partner selected. What we also see more and more frequently now is that the solution has already been chosen and the customer's selection process becomes a matter of finding the right partner.

When choosing a partner, one may think that the criteria under which it is evaluated have to do with price, competence, experience, references, and added value, but I would contend that the biggest criterion is perceived risk.

Deploying an ERP system is a significant business project that will put a tremendous amount of stress on your organization, both financially and against your human resources. Selecting the wrong software or partner can be very costly. Consciously or not, management will most likely pick the solution/vendor combination that appears to be the least risky.

The crux of it then resides in the evaluation of risk. How do you evaluate this risk? Which criteria do you consider?

First, let us debunk one belief: bigger is not always better. Larger partners may seem more secure at first glance, but quality should be more important than quantity. Depending on the size of your organization and project, it may be true that a certain size partner is required. After all, you need to make sure that your vendor has the necessary bandwidth to support your project. Please note, however, that for me, quality also means culture.

As an organization grows, it becomes more difficult to achieve a high degree of commitment from all its employees; maintaining the same level of quality across the board can be challenging. A strong mission and vibrant culture will help mitigate these troubles.

Larger organizations usually offer structured support services comprised of a dedicated team: you may benefit from their additional depth, but you may also find yourself competing with their other clients for attention. Well-trained ERP consultants are difficult to find and keep. They are expensive. If you are not a high-profile or high-paying customer, you may not be assigned these top-notch consultants but only their less experienced colleagues.

A smaller partner will often demonstrate more nimbleness, provide a more personalized service, and offer a more concentrated pool of experience. You may even get to deal with the owner directly. Chances are you will get knowledgeable resources at a lower cost, provided they are available when you need them.

If you decide to go with a smaller partner, you could very well be getting their full attention and personal touch, but you still want to assess your risk should they lose an employee assigned to you or, God forbid, if the owner decides he has had enough and wants to go raise sheep on a farm.

In all circumstances, ask those prospective partners for references, and follow up on them. No one will provide you with poor references, but contacting them could provide more insight into the nature and personality of your vendor on how they deal with adversity and support their customers.

Ultimately, make sure you are a significant customer to your partner. Match their size to yours, but also validate that their culture fits yours. You are going into this for the long haul. I believe Tom Demarco's saying also applies here: "Get the right people. Then no matter what else you might do wrong after that, the people will save you. That's what management is all about."

Case Study

I would have quite a few anecdotes to share on this topic as more than 30 percent of our existing customers have decided to change partners and work with us. I will limit myself to three while mixing it up a bit as you're about to find out.

The first story is about our very first Microsoft customer. They had deployed an older version of the ERP solution we knew and sold. The original work had been done by a vendor who was not familiar with manufacturing, and wanting to implement that functionality a few years later, they selected another vendor who had the expertise to help them out. That large vendor, owned and backed by a company listed on the stock market, seemed like the right partner to work with, yet the project team that was put together failed.

Over time, knowledge of the original customizations had eroded, and to compound problems, they were now on the other side of a failed deployment with an aging version of the application. It was decided that they would carefully go out and look for a third partner. During that process, we were able to differentiate ourselves by being candid about the situation and making harsh, but honest recommendations. They selected us to completely re-implement the solution, and the rest is history.

The second anecdote still hurts. A few years ago, we went through a lengthy, time-consuming, and difficult presales cycle with a prospect whom we convinced Dynamics 365 Business Central was the right solution for them. My team and I spent at least a hundred hours working on this deal, and we felt good about our understanding of their challenges and our ability to deliver their project.

Alas, at the very last minute, the prospect chose to go elsewhere. (Whaaat?) I don't think this was ethical and wise—I am clearly biased—but it does prove my point that finding the right partner is important. At least they got that right!

My last recounting has to do with a project I heard about recently. A reseller grossly underestimated an implementation effort and ended up in a bind to deliver.

I am told their decision was to pull multiple resources from other projects and assign them to the big one to get it through the finish line. As you can expect, their other clients suffered collateral damage.

I don't have enough information to judge whether this was the right call or not. I suspect the risk of not delivering the large project was significant to the vendor. Legally significant. I suppose it could potentially happen to anyone, but how would you feel if you were one of their smaller clients?

SECTION 3

PLANNING THE PROJECT

PROJECT PLANNING

If you fail to plan, you plan to fail.

—Vijay Dhameliya

> **Key Takeaway: The more time and resources you reasonably spend planning your project, the more likely you are to succeed.**

Antoine de Saint-Exupéry said it well: "A goal without a plan is just a wish." It may seem obvious, but small and medium businesses can sometimes cut corners, too caught up in the enthusiasm of entrepreneurship. Project planning is a very important early phase of project management. The bigger the project, the bigger the plan.

The discipline of project planning involves defining a project charter and measurable objectives, identifying deliverables, planning the schedule, and formulating appropriate supporting plans. During the proposal phase, a statement of work should regroup these elements into one deliverable. These components of the plan should be further detailed and fleshed out by the project managers once the project begins.

Project Charter

The project charter essentially describes who is involved in the project and what their roles and responsibilities will be. Resources from both organizations, client and vendor, come together to form the project team. The steering committee, project sponsors, project managers, functional analysts, super users, developers, and anyone else implicated will be identified, as they are all constituents of the project team.

The steering committee is an essential part of the project charter. The steering committee is usually comprised of the project sponsor, project leaders, and key decision-makers from both organizations. The role of the steering committee is to oversee the project, assess progress, and make key decisions, such as deciding on the relevance of customizations or the acceptance of scope changes.

Objectives

Your first objective when defining project objectives should be to define objectives that are identifiable and measurable. *(Yes, I did this on purpose.)* They are typically derived from your business case and often represent a series of weaknesses you plan to eliminate or opportunities you hope to capture with the new application. These will be the benchmarks by which you determine the success of your project.

It may be difficult to come up with measurable objectives. It's okay to have some qualitative goals. It's better than not having goals at all. *(My youngest son didn't have goals in high school, so he ended up improving his beer pong skills.)*

Deliverables

There can be many project deliverables for each phase of the project, but some examples are fit-gap analysis, communications plan, user guides, custom code, migration scripts, and oh yes, a working ERP software to run your business with. It is important to identify and decide what the deliverables of your project will be, since they will remain with you as documentation after the completion of the project and also serve as triggers for quality sign-offs. They will vary based on the context and complexity of your deployment: larger projects usually imply more control requirements and more documentation.

We will discuss some of these in later chapters.

Timeline

A very important aspect of any project is the timeline. Tools like Gantt and PERT charts are often used, but on small projects, an Excel spreadsheet can get the job done. This aspect of project planning will be discussed further in an upcoming chapter.

Below is a list of common tasks you should find in your ERP deployment plan.

- Installation and kickoff
- Business review or process reengineering
- Workshops (configuration, tests, and training)
- User guides
- Data migration
- Customizations
- Security configuration and testing
- Test scripts
- Integrated testing
- End-user training
- Go-live
- Support

Supporting Plans

An ERP implementation implies plans within plans. The project plan typically includes other plans that help support the execution efforts, such as a training plan, communication plan, testing plan, etc. We will discuss the communication plan in the "Change Management" chapter.

Depending on your deployment strategy, training can happen in different project phases. We like to train super users first, using functional workshops, making them comfortable with the solution as soon as possible. This promotes knowledge transfer and reinforces their role and responsibilities as key users.

In our methodology, your super users become the trainers of your end users. For each of these training efforts, it is good to identify the participants, topics covered, and timeline. Another benefit of training plans is that they may be used as supporting documentation in the event your organization is eligible for training subsidies.

Testing plans are used to identify areas, sequence, and timing of testing activities, which is the general aspect of the plan. When diving down into details, test scripts will be written to identify software features that need to be tested and their expected results.

Sample documents can be found here: www.erphelp.co/downloadables.

Case Study

Simon was wondering what was going wrong. He was working extremely hard to make this project successful. They were doing their best to adapt the system to their specific requirements and deliver a great solution. He had not received the backing he expected from the top brass, and he often felt like he was going against the wind. Still, he believed this was not enough to explain the countless delays and problems that seemed to come out of nowhere.

His vendor had supplied him with a very responsive and qualified consultant who, on top of that, was assigned only to their project and thus was totally available. Lack of resources could not explain the issues and certainly not any lack of motivation. He needed some help figuring this out. He remembered meeting this great guy one day who had given him a book he had written about ERP projects and decided to give it a shot, in the off chance he could learn something.

Something magical happened! (Yup! I have this effect on people.) *Like waters parting in front of Moses or Newton getting hit on the head by an apple, he realized what was missing: project planning!*

Okay, this fictitious anecdote was in the first edition of my book but interesting enough—I think—to remain in this second edition. I would be remiss if I did not add some insight based on my experience.

As I pointed out previously, project planning is a very important activity that should not be underestimated. What I have seen happen from time to time, and that you might want to keep on your radar, are the following mistakes:

- *Underestimating effort, which includes assigning people who do not have enough availability to be totally effective.*
- *Building a timeline that is based on a go-live date that someone drew from a hat. (I am quite convinced it has happened at least once to somebody.)*
- *Activities that are not appropriately documented.*
- *Blurry objectives.*
- *Lack of leadership. If you are the business owner, stay on top of things. Delegate, but oversee.*

IDENTIFY OBJECTIVES

Begin with the end in mind.

—Stephen Covey

> **Key Takeaway: Clear objectives will help you plan, execute, and ultimately measure success.**

As mentioned in the previous chapter, your objectives should be identifiable and measurable. They are often expressed as key performance indicators.

"Replacing our old accounting software" is too general to be an effective goal, just like "running the hundred-meter race" is too vague for Andre De Grasse. Even "winning an Olympic medal" is not precise enough. Both statements will be appropriately redefined by a clear objective such as "running the 100-meter race in 9.85 seconds." Not only would De Grasse know that running in 9.85 seconds should be good enough to give him a medal, but he also knows it would be his personal best.

Moreover, training to run the 100-meter race is not quite the same as training to run the 100-meter race in 9.85 seconds. The level of planning, preparation, and dedication required to achieve this precise goal is much higher. Jesse Owens, Olympic gold-medalist, said, "We all have dreams. In order to make dreams come into reality, it takes an awful lot of determination, dedication, self-discipline, and effort." Your project goals are your organization's dreams. *(I love this example. Very witty and clear. Probably not my original idea.)*

In many instances, organizations have not yet defined reliable KPIs. Depending on the state of your current business and software applications, it may be difficult to calculate viable key performance indicators (KPIs) to set your objectives. KPIs require good data to be effective, and yours may be disseminated across an accounting package, two other software solutions, and multiple spreadsheets. If this is your situation, try to do your best and calculate indicators that can provide insight into your current and future operational performance. Have faith that your new ERP system should help you define better KPIs in the near future.

Some examples of KPIs are the following:

- **Inventory turnover**—measuring how many times per year your organization is able to sell its entire inventory
- **Average inventory**—measuring the average value of inventory over a defined time period
- **On-time delivery**—measuring complete on-time deliveries to customers
- **Rate of return**—measuring the rate of returned items and the reasons behind it

Some of your objectives may also be related to your project execution rather than your business operations. Your budget is an important KPI you should include in your success measurements.

Once you have determined what indicators will bear witness to the level of quality of your new system, you may also need to take multiple measurements over time to allow for a reasonable stabilization period and to ensure your post-deployment levels of operational efficiency are maintained or even improved as months pass by.

System stabilization will be discussed in a later chapter.

Case Study

As his company was about to embark on the ERP deployment train, Mark was trying to come up with clear, measurable objectives for his project team. Not an easy task, considering that their legacy system was a small basic accounting package complemented by Excel. Where do you get key performance indicators when you can barely get any data out of your system? Net benefit before income tax didn't seem sufficient.

Mark opted for a few qualitative goals that included effectively replacing their old system and deploying a few new modules. Implementing within budget and the allocated time frame were obvious targets. Since the business could not currently rely on perpetual inventory and proper production planning, reducing stock levels over a certain time frame became a measurable goal. The stabilization period was set to six months after their go-live.

It was also decided that as soon as the new ERP system was in place, a series of KPIs would be implemented and measured over time to promote a constant improvement of the company's performance.

HANDLE THE SCOPE

Deciding what not to do is as important as deciding
what to do.

—Steve Jobs

> **Key Takeaway: Proper planning includes appro-
> priate and tight handling of scope. Scope creep is
> a cancer you must avoid.**

Defining and handling project scope is a very important project
management task. The larger the scope, the longer the timeline.
The larger the scope, the higher the budget. The larger the scope,
the higher the risk. The larger the scope, the shorter your walk
on the plank. *(I was on a roll here and really fell in love with the
formula.)*

It is very easy to get carried away and take on more than one can
chew. This is also true of organizations, even more so successful
organizations: prior success does not necessarily guarantee you
will succeed again, especially if your success is not related to
ERP implementation. Deploying a new warehouse, creating a new
product, or making an acquisition are all important and significant
business endeavors, but they are not the same as implementing
ERP software.

A good dose of humility is required when planning an ERP
implementation because it is very easy to underestimate the effort
that will be required. After all, the devil is in the details, and you
cannot possibly foresee all issues that may arise. Think of it as
renovating a centennial home: you are bound to hit a few surprises.
Be careful to avoid optimism bias.

Bill Gates judiciously said, "Most people overestimate what they can do in one year and underestimate what they can do in ten years." *(Since your ERP project should not take ten years—OMG!— then you should expect to be too optimistic.)*

On top of that, an ERP project often affects all or nearly all the departments in the company: this creates much stress on the firm and its people. It is not uncommon that internal political pressures impact the scope.

In his book, *ERP Demystified*, Alexis Leon mentions that "extracting and cleansing the data from the existing system can be the single largest task in the project." Technology makes this job easier nowadays, but the statement still illustrates how tricky certain steps can be. Reporting requirements should not be underestimated either.

For all these reasons, and more, we suggest Auren Hoffman's advice: "Limit it in scope. Make it simple. Get success. Then iterate." Whenever possible, cutting your full scope into smaller phases and getting quicker wins is a better approach to getting user buy-ins, getting faster benefits, and improving your deployment skills as an organization.

In a DIY project, renovating your home one room at a time is much easier than gutting the entire house and doing everything at once. Especially if you live in it, like your business.

Case Study

Stories related to this topic also abound! Quite a few times in my career, I have worked on projects where the scope was poorly managed, mostly because the requirements were not properly identified up front. An unclear vision of the objectives to attain means an ill-defined scope, which makes the project susceptible to scope creep, especially if there are customizations involved. This can even happen on smaller projects. If your project becomes a huge prototyping exercise, you are in for the long haul.

Another typical case of poorly managed scope I have seen has to do with the potential disconnect between a vendor's sales and services departments. Salespeople, by and large, really, really want to sell. So they do. I remember this specific project I was once stuck in. It was sold as a four-month pipe dream but ended up being a nine-month roller-coaster ride that sucked the life out of me.

This is one of the reasons why I perform most of the sales and presales activities at my company. I want a former consultant, not a salesperson, doing this. After all, we are specialists, not furniture salesmen. Even then, it remains difficult to estimate efforts and define a good scope. In presales, you are still working at a higher altitude. Implementing an ERP solution follows deductive reasoning—a logical approach where you progress from general ideas to specific conclusions. (Here I go with this university quote again. Culture is like jam.)

DEFINE THE BUDGET

A budget tells us what we can't afford, but it doesn't keep us from buying it.

—William Feather

Key Takeaway: Realistic and detailed project planning is paramount to effective budget management.

Budget management is intimately tied to your scope and objectives. Limiting your scope has the important and non-negligible benefit of limiting your budget. *(Tell me, would you rather spend money on a Corvette or a software package?)*

Kidding aside, there clearly is value to be gained by deploying an ERP system if you have built a solid business case for it and engaged your company on this path. The value is ultimately driven by your objectives and the return on investment they represent for you.

Your budget must realistically reflect the efforts needed to get you where you want to go. Due diligence is mandatory, and too much optimism could be detrimental to your health, mental or otherwise. Detailed planning will not guarantee a perfect budget, but it will get you much closer to where you need to be. Add some contingency to the mix, and you should be increasing your accuracy significantly.

This all sounds simple enough, yet surveys show that 54 percent of ERP projects go over budget. Why is it that budgets are so hard to respect when deploying ERP?

Unicity

Your company is unique *(like every other company out there)*. It is true that most companies share many, many common functions and requirements, yet every company has a little je ne sais quoi that makes it unique. That X factor is a differentiator, and each ERP project has its share of unknowns. This uncertainty represents a budgeting risk.

Scope

Granted, no one has a crystal ball when it comes to the evaluation of scope, but as we discussed in the previous chapter, it is still very common to experience scope creep in an ERP project. The problems are not only underestimating effort and poor planning, but also perhaps related to the intense competition in the market. As vendors vie for your favors, they will work very hard to look as appealing to you as possible, and consciously or not, they might reduce the price tag of their proposal to win your business.

If they do not reduce the price of software or their rate, then guess what gets reduced? Right, the budgeted hours. You can negotiate the price of the software and the service rates, but ultimately, you want to make sure the overall budget is realistic and your vendor's assumptions make sense!

Customizations

Customizations can easily get out of hand and riddle your well-planned budget with so many holes your ship will sink like the *Titanic*. Customizations should be kept to a minimum and should only be justifiable if they impart your business with a clear edge over your competitors, address a mandatory regulatory requirement, or perhaps provide you with some other clear advantage.

Integrating your ERP with other systems can also prove tricky. When working on proposals, we are regularly called to estimate the cost of an interface without having enough details. That is risky for both the vendor and the customer.

Try to adapt your operations to the application unless the processes involved nullify what distinguishes your business from its competitors. In other words, as long as you are you, the rest does not matter so much.

Every customization should be challenged considering its return on investment: if you cannot demonstrate its usefulness, you do not need it.

The Right Solution

Finding the right solution has a direct impact on your budget: midsized businesses should stay away from the most expensive tier 1 solutions, aimed at enterprise-scaled companies. There are now very deep and flexible tier 2 solutions that can meet most of your requirements. Numerous vertical solutions have also been developed and are now offered on the market.

Case Study

Let us revisit the case mentioned in the previous chapter since budget, scope, and timeline are all connected. We'll call it the pipe dream project. Sometimes, for various reasons, such as having to live with unfair and unrealistic expectations coming from top management, or lack of ERP experience, some executives will be vulnerable to fantasy stories.

In this pipe dream project, the customer was sold a four-to-five-month implementation that—listen to this—involved three manufacturing plants with a tremendous amount of stockkeeping units and production recipes. Moreover, the business had been using a customized legacy system for about twenty years! Users were set in their ways; data migration was an enormous challenge; and their manufacturing operations were diversified enough to create significant challenges. Conclusion—deployment time multiplied by two, budget blown away...and people losing their jobs.

While some projects will be difficult and complex due to their nature, others don't have to be. Aiming to reduce the risk of implementation for some of our customers, we have introduced fixed-bid deployments. This tends to work well for smaller companies, and the primary condition is that we must deploy a vanilla version of the solution. Customizations and integrations are not fixed bids, but at least the client achieves peace of mind for some of the work.

A vanilla version, *or* vanilla implementation, *means that the standard functionality of the solution is used. The system is deployed as is.*

CONTROL TIME

Time is more valuable than money. You can get more money, but you cannot get more time.

—Jim Rohn

> **Key Takeaway: Time, a rare asset, needs to be managed effectively if you want to ensure the success of your project.**

Have you heard this one, "Chuck Norris doesn't wear a watch, he simply decides what time it is"? Sadly, you are not Chuck Norris, and therefore, you must manage and control your time very well. Along with scope and budget, time is the third pillar that needs to be balanced and supervised by effective project management.

It is not easy for anyone to anticipate the future. As you plan your project, you must do your best to evaluate the tasks that are required and the time to accomplish them. Any project worth the name should include a project schedule. To do so, you can rely on scheduling tools, like Gantt or PERT charts.

Gantt Chart

A Gantt chart is a graphical scheduling tool devised by Henry Gantt in the 1910s. His idea must have been pure genius if we are still using it today. The tasks are listed from top to bottom, and each is represented by a bar across a timeline. For each task, start and end dates are tracked as well as the relationships that exist between each task.

You can find multiple Gantt software on the market. I believe Microsoft Project may be the most popular.

You can find an example of a Gantt chart used in the deployment of an ERP solution here: www.erphelp.co/downloadables.

One of the project manager's responsibilities is to maintain the Gantt chart and keep track of the completion of each task. Whenever an activity takes more time than expected, it could impact your timeline if the activity is on the critical path. The critical path is defined as the longest sequence of tasks that must be completed to finish a project. These tasks are called critical activities. In other words, these are the tasks that are sequentially dependent on one another. Some tasks can be done simultaneously and are thus called parallel tasks. One task that must be completed before another one starts is called a prerequisite task. So if a prerequisite task on the critical path runs late, the whole project runs late.

What can you do when that happens? You can hope that other critical activities will take less time to complete so you can make up for lost time. If your project manager included contingency in the plan, then you have some buffer to work with. Otherwise, you may need to reduce your scope or...cancel vacations! *(Just kidding, of course.)*

Aside from the time each task requires to be completed, your schedule should take into consideration the number of days each resource can devote to the project, including when they will be away on vacation. You should also incorporate peak stress times for the organization, such as cyclical rush periods, as they can really affect your timeline if people must focus on other important operational tasks. In the end, the effort required to accomplish your project will certainly differ from its planned duration.

PERT Chart

A PERT chart is also a graphical scheduling tool used for project management. PERT is a methodology developed by the US Navy in the 1950s to manage the Polaris submarine missile program, and its acronym means program evaluation review technique.

With this approach, tasks are represented by arrows that end at nodes. The nodes represent milestones while diverging arrows represent parallel paths. A PERT chart looks like a sideways flowchart, and project duration is calculated by adding the time of all milestones within the longest path.

I have not worked with a PERT chart when I was managing projects and implementing ERP, yet I thought introducing the concept might prove valuable to you, my beloved reader. A very simple example is shown below.

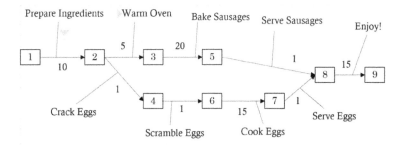

Numbered rectangles indicate a milestone.
Directional arrows represent tasks, diverging arrows parallel tasks.

SECTION 4

EXECUTION

PROJECT MANAGEMENT

Trying to manage a project without project management is like trying to play a football game without a game plan.

—K. Tate

Key Takeaway: Project management is the underestimated art of driving your team toward an established common goal.

According to Wikipedia, project management is the discipline of initiating, planning, executing, controlling, and closing the work of a team to achieve specific goals and meet specific success criteria.

Simply put, project management is everything you need to do to make sure things get done! I am being facetious...but not really. Management of projects requires a structured approach, tools, and methods that are meticulously applied to make sure something intended to happen effectively happens. A project manager is an overseer, but also a communicator and a diplomat.

Ask any project manager, and he will tell you project management in the information technology world is a lot like herding cattle in the great Canadian Prairies. Well, maybe not in those specific terms, but much of it has to do with focusing people on the path you need them to take to get project tasks accomplished. Project managers can sometimes annoy people, but as Harvey Mackay reminds us, "Deadlines aren't bad. They help you organize your time. They help you set priorities. They make you get going when you might not feel like it."

If you've read *The 7 Habits of Highly Successful People* by Stephen Covey, you'll understand what I mean when I say project management falls in quadrant II. Quadrant II is the organizing quadrant. It represents time invested in planning, orchestrating, and preparing so that things run more smoothly later.

Jean de la Fontaine wrote, *"Rien ne sert de courir, il faut partir à point."* Slow and steady wins the race.

Large projects usually benefit from a structured approach to project management. Larger organizations tend to incorporate project management into their culture and do not mind spending the money to properly manage their projects. They understand that poor project management can lead to disastrous results, regardless of the project's nature; that is how full-time positions for project managers are created.

At the other end of the spectrum, you find companies, usually small- and medium-sized businesses, who believe formal project management is not really required for smaller projects. Small projects can be assigned to managers as an additional task on their plate, no biggie. The problem that may arise from such an approach, however, is that project management requires great focus, and when it is just another task among many, that focus gets diluted.

What does insufficient focus entail? Well, as Frederick Brooks would say, "How does a project get to be a year late? One day at a time."

Although project management helps you stay focused, adaptability remains important: apply the tools of the trade but be nimble; change direction as needed to circumvent obstacles. A project is by nature very unpredictable, and so you must be able to adapt. Most people, and Google, attribute this quote to Anthony Robbins: "If you always do what you've always done, you'll always get what you always got."

We already discussed the planning aspects of project management in the previous section. We will discuss more aspects related to execution when we cover deployment methodology, budget control, and change management in upcoming chapters. The most important aspect of project management to remember is that it is not something you deal with in passing; it is a fundamental component of your successful deployment.

Case Study

Project management is often overlooked in small and medium businesses. If a project culture is nonexistent, you will often find that the benefits of project management are grossly underestimated. I have come across this situation a few times in my career. It typically goes like this.

George (his real name will remain undisclosed to protect the innocent) *figured that he would handle project management duties. As the finance director and project sponsor, it would be a natural extension of his role. It would also save the company money. A no-brainer.*

Three months of self-induced pain later, George's project was in disarray and seemed stalled. Not having the time to perform appropriate project management activities, the whole thing had become a study in improvisation. Project members were having to fill in the gaps, pulling things in different directions.

George, feeling like a candle in the wind, hired a part-time project manager before burning out. (Did you hear Elton John's song in your head as you read the last sentence?)

BUSINESS PROCESS REVIEW

If you can't describe what you are doing as a
process, you don't know what you're doing.
　　　　　　　　　　　　　—W. Edwards Deming

**Key Takeaway: Understanding and optimizing
how you operate your business is more important than the tools being utilized to get the work
done.**

Business processes are all the activities your organization must
perform to accomplish its primary goal: deliver a service or product
to its customers. Business processes are often segregated into
specific business flows for better understanding, such as order to
cash, plan to produce, or procure to pay.

Business processes are like the habits and quirks we develop as
human beings. *(Most of you have them, right? I'm asking because
I can't find any for myself.)* We often do not even realize we have
them until someone points them out to us, or until we take the
time to evaluate our own behavior. If a corporation does not spend
the required time and energy to define or document its business
processes, as Deming puts it, it doesn't know what it's doing. This
ongoing activity is called business process management.

I have often seen companies launch themselves into an ERP
deployment without a clear understanding of their business
processes. Executives often balk at the additional cost. This can
be detrimental during the design phase, as the collective business
knowledge is in people's heads, and as we all know, everyone's
head is a different landscape. This often leads to lengthy

discussions and debates that could be avoided with appropriately documented processes.

A business process review is only possible if you have documented your processes before kicking off your implementation. A review will thus consist of mapping the business flows to your newly acquired ERP solution. The entire project team will benefit from working with this documentation.

Moreover, as you contemplate the use of your new ERP solution, you possess the opportunity to rethink how you work and introduce new efficiencies made possible by the new application. Using today's technology, you can introduce automation and optimizations that can help you gain an edge over your competitors. As the adage goes, "Change your life by changing yourself."

If your processes have not yet been documented, then there isn't much to review. If you are still in the design phase of your implementation, it would be beneficial to extend that phase so you can properly document your processes, even if they are closely mapped to your vanilla solution.

There are multiple techniques to choose from when you want to map your processes. Some of the most commonly used are business process modeling notation (BPMN) created for that specific purpose, easy-to-use flowcharts, and UML diagrams.

It's never too late to document your processes, even after go-live. This exercise will better align your operations with your goals, improve control over your activities and resources, increase productivity by diminishing inefficiencies, and ultimately improve your products or services.

What has helped McDonald's grow the way it has in its decades of existence was its business system—the use of standardized processes designed to reduce costs by maximizing efficiency.

Case Study

Remember the four-month pipe dream project I mentioned in a previous chapter...the one that ended up a nine-month roller-coaster ride that sucked the life out of me? Well, that project also did not have documented business processes.

The users and IT personnel assigned to the implementation team were very knowledgeable as they had been with the company a long time and had accumulated much knowledge about its operations over the years.

Despite the strength of the team, it was hard to extract and interpret all that information. I visited the manufacturing plants. We conducted multiple workshops. We tested multiple scenarios in the system.

I believe we might have been able to save time, or at least construct a realistic initial project scope, if processes had been documented from the day the ERP selection process began.

METHODOLOGY

Nothing is particularly hard if you divide it into small jobs.

—Henry Ford

Key Takeaway: Methodology is a structured approach to project management that helps create order out of chaos.

Ward Cunningham said, "I don't claim to be a methodologist, but I act like one only because I do methodology to protect myself from crazy methodologists." He has a point: methodology should be helping you, not hindering you. It is therefore important to choose the right methodology and apply it with enough flexibility so that you can manage your project optimally. Methodology is not an end in itself but an approach and a set of tools to help you with project management and execution.

Implementing ERP without a methodology is akin to building IKEA furniture without reading the assembly instructions: doable, but clearly risky. *(With experience, it is sometimes possible to ease up a bit on the documentation and paperwork. This is how I became an IKEA hacker!)*

Deployment projects need to be separated into steps, or phases, where each step produces a set of deliverables. These steps tend to be similar from project to project, but the deliverables may vary. Our approach to implementing ERP is typically composed of the following phases:

Diagnostic

The sales cycle, represented by Section 1 of this book and composed of presales activities such as discovery and demonstration, is really the first phase of your project. Consultative selling is mandatory in our domain. There are so many moving parts and various aspects to understand that we must share information and knowledge from the very beginning.

The most important deliverable you should expect out of this phase is a proposal, or statement of work. A return on investment may also be included, but I don't come across this very much in my daily professional life. Companies tend to work on this by themselves.

Planning

The planning phase was fully covered in Section 2. During this start-up phase, the project team and the steering committee will be formed. A kickoff meeting will be conducted. The main deliverable is a project charter.

Analysis

The analysis phase is often melded into the design phase, but if not, it will involve a business review, and the typical deliverables will be a list of business requirements, a fit-gap analysis document, and perhaps revised business process workflows.

This phase helps our consultants figure out what features of the system should be configured, tested, and shown to the super users. Your core team is composed of people dubbed as super users, and they help the consultants configure the application to meet the previously identified business requirements. It really is a preparation step as we are not yet in the nitty-gritty aspects of the implementation. *(We call them super users because they are supposed to be better than the rest, not because they have superpowers—unless you consider being proficient at computers a superpower. For some people, I guess it is.)*

Implementing an ERP system is an iterative project where each loop is more refined than the previous one. We are always working from the general to the specific. *(It's gotta be an obsessive-compulsive disorder. I just can't help it.)*

Design

The design phase is used to train your core team so they become the receptacles of knowledge and expertise within the organization. At the same time, your super users return the favor by teaching the functional consultants about your business.

These workshops are essential in determining how the system will run in your environment, with your business rules. In this step, we are mapping your business processes to the system.

New functional gaps may be discovered during functional work-shops, and the fit-gap analysis document gets updated with this new information.

Other deliverables usually include functional documents describing how the system will be configured and used.

Development

Whenever applicable, the development phase will focus on cus-tomizing the application, creating reports, interfacing with external systems, and preparing migration scripts. This phase is obviously more technical in nature, but the core team can work on develop-ing specific user guides and functional test scripts while the pro-grammers ply their trade. *(Just slide them sandwiches under the door, and they will do just fine.)*

Communication between the functional consultants, super users, and the technical team is ongoing during this step to make sure what is coded meets the requirements. Programmers will unit-test their work while consultants and super users should perform functional testing on any customized feature.

Integrated Testing

Also called the conference room pilot, this phase is crucial as everything comes together for final testing and approval. *(Everything is crucial in an ERP deployment. Using the word crucial can also become an OCD.)* Simply put, the conference room pilot is a go-live simulation. Run the system from end to end, and make sure it can handle the most important business scenarios depicted by the test scripts.

During this phase, we are not testing customizations or features, but entire processes such as procure to pay, plan to produce, order to cash, record to report, etc.

Is the system ready and fully functional? Corrective measures will certainly be applied following these tests, but the final goal is to assess the risk of going live, and if everything looks good enough, make the call.

Go-Live Preparation

This step obviously precedes the activation of the system. End users get trained by the core team. The user guides come in handy for this. The final task checklist is put together and reviewed to make sure it is all-encompassing. *(People cancel their vacation, and a good delivery place is selected. We recommend pizza for the increase in morale it brings and because it can be eaten quickly.)*

Go-Live

This is it—the big (long) weekend. Depending on the nature of your business, inventory is counted, and final data migrations occur. Ongoing projects are carried over, manufacturing orders are transferred, and all sorts of cutoff operations take place. Much work is also being performed in the accounting department to make sure all is in balance and the books reflect reality after data loads and other important activities have taken place.

When the okay is given, the new system is turned on, and a new life begins. Do you smell the roses and feel the sun shining on your skin? Perhaps this warmth you're feeling is in fact your body temperature increasing as cortisol is being produced by your stressed mind. This pressure you're facing is common and normal. The work is not over.

Please note that Murphy—from Murphy's Law—will always try to make an appearance and mess things up. He usually does not limit himself to the proverbial buttered toast. Anything that can go wrong will go wrong...eventually.

Transactions will be botched, work will pile up, and users will find creative ways to use the system that no one could have ever imagined. *(You've heard the adage: "Make something idiotproof, and they will make a better idiot.")*

This is why integrated testing is so important. The more issues you catch upstream, the less arduous your deployment will be. Your users have been trained, but they are not experienced yet, as any young car driver coming out of driving school can attest. *(I could rant about drivers here, but I will restrain myself.)*

Support

The support phase begins when you are operating the system. The effort required will depend on many variables, such as how many users are utilizing the system, the complexity of your operations, the readiness of your team, etc. You may need help to get through your first month-end process. There is a normal period of stabilization following any go-live, so make sure you have planned and budgeted for that.

❖ ❖ ❖

As was mentioned earlier, the methodology must be flexible and adaptable to your reality. Phases can be merged, but the underlying tasks still need to be accomplished. The area where adaptation eligibility exists is mostly with the deliverables. You can decide on their format and their verbosity. Will it be a point-form spreadsheet or a full-fledged technical document?

Some vendors, typically the large ones, will often promote a turnkey approach. With this methodology, the effort is more on the vendor's shoulders than on your team's. In this case, the analysis, design, and development phases are mostly performed by the vendor, and your people's participation is somewhat limited to providing input on the existing business processes.

Once this step is completed, the vendor conducts a prototype review where your people are educated on the new solution and adjustments are made as required. Once the prototype is complete, the conference room pilot takes place, followed by the other regular phases.

Both approaches have pros and cons, and those should be evaluated carefully before they are applied. The traditional method— which we favor—has the benefit of helping your organization take ownership of the system, of its processes and data, but it can be taxing on your human resources, especially if the people on the core team do not possess ERP experience. Leaning more on your vendor has the benefit of freeing up your employees and putting more responsibility on the consultants, but user acceptance may become an issue if the vendor's solution is perceived as theirs, not yours.

Agile Methodology

We hear a lot about Agile methodology these days, and so I think it is worth a discussion. The Agile theorem, as I will call it, saw its birth when a few people got together and drafted a new set of values related to the management of software development. It goes something like this:

- Individuals and interactions over processes and tools
- Working software over comprehensive documentation
- Customer collaboration over contract negotiation
- Responding to change over following a plan

While there is value in the items on the right, we value the items on the left more.

Kelly Waters, author of the book *All about Agile*, has listed ten key principles that make Agile fundamentally different from traditional software development methods. Let us comment briefly on them, within the specific context of ERP projects.

1. **Active user involvement is imperative.**
   The traditional method of relying on and elevating super user skills within the core team embraces this principle fully.
2. **The team must be empowered to make decisions.**
   Depending on who is assigned to the core team, it can be very effective to allow them to make as many key decisions as they can.
3. **Requirements evolve, but the timescale is fixed.**
   This statement refers to scope management. Instead of trying to include all known requirements in the original scope of the project to make sure nothing is forgotten and then get approval for unexpected changes, this principle enforces a fixed timeline with variable deliveries.
   One example of how this principle can be applied is by prioritizing customizations and delivering only those that do not impact the project timeline. Another use case would be to postpone the deployment of some features or modules to later phases. Fixed assets, material maintenance,

and finite scheduling are good examples of modules that may not be included in phase 1.

4. **Capture requirements at a high level, lightweight and visual.**

   This principle consists of further defining requirements as work progresses, remaining flexible so as not to engage in a dead end. This applies more to development, in my humble opinion, than it does to ERP deployments, but the implementation of an ERP system remains an exercise, as we mentioned earlier, that originates from the general and evolves toward the specific. *(OMG! Sorry!)* Requirements identified early in the selection process are usually further detailed in the workshops. Still, you need a solid minimum to make sure you select and then configure the system properly.

5. **Develop small, incremental releases, and iterate.**

   This principle is interesting from the perspective of scope management and ties in with the fixed timescale. Quick returns on investments and smaller deliverables are easier to manage than large, big-bang projects. If possible, "divide and conquer" is the way to go.

6. **Focus on frequent delivery of products.**

   In our context, this is the same as number 5.

7. **Complete each feature before moving on to the next.**

   - This is an interesting principle. In software development, the whole team will be focused on completing and fully testing a feature before moving on to the next one. Proceeding in this manner keeps everyone focused while promoting teamwork. When a feature is done, it is really done. This means the iteration, called a sprint, is complete. Case closed.

   - In ERP projects, the system being deployed is fully integrated and affects most business areas. Keeping a holistic approach is necessary, but each deliverable and each phase should be fully completed when declared as such. This way, momentum is maintained, and the focus is on the task ahead.

8. **Apply the 80/20 rule.**

   Pareto's principle can be applied in most areas of life, including project management. Prioritizing customizations immediately comes to mind. Applying our focus on the most important changes for the organization, and not wasting time on events—exceptions really—that happen three days per year, will prevent scope creep.

   Other hypotheses that can be derived from Pareto law are the following:

   - That 80 percent of the value your company receives from software comes from 20 percent of the software's functionality.
   - That 80 percent of the software's standard functionality should work fine in your organization. Customizations should not exceed 20 percent.
   - That 20 percent of the implementation cost will get you 80 percent of the functionality.
   - That fixing the top 20 percent of software errors would result in addressing 80 percent of reported software issues.

9. **Testing is integrated throughout the project life cycle—test early and often.**

   This principle is a bit difficult to apply in ERP deployments, since all efforts lead to the conference room pilot where the system will be tested as a whole. There is great dependency between its various components, and testing each piece individually, be it a standard feature or a custom one, remains limiting.

   Still, concerns about quality should be applied to every project deliverable so that integrated testing becomes much simpler down the road. Customizations should be thoroughly tested, and we will address this topic in an upcoming chapter.

10. **A collaborative and cooperative approach between all stakeholders is essential.**

    Given the adaptive nature of the Agile approach, collaboration is deemed crucial (*crucial!*) for the attainment of success. I would contend that the moment you work on anything that requires more than one person's involvement, collaboration and cooperation should be mandatory and promoted. This one's a no-brainer.

If you think there may be issues tied to collaboration during your implementation, I suggest reading *The Five Dysfunctions of a Team* by Patrick Lencioni. You will find great principles in his book that can be leveraged to greatly improve teamwork in any environment.

Although the abovementioned key principles apply primarily to software development, some of them can be integrated within a traditional waterfall ERP deployment approach. After all, one of the main objectives of Agile is to respond to the unpredictability of project management, which is a determining challenge of almost any ERP implementation project.

Case Study

Using a robust implementation methodology is so important that software manufacturers who, as part of their business model, partner with value-added resellers to sell and deploy their products often create their own methodology. Microsoft has created Sure Step, a methodology they promote within the partner channel through training and certification requirements.

It may seem obvious to all that a good methodology will save time and money, but on the flip side, it also has a cost. I have experienced implementations where documentation was not seen as valuable and was therefore kept to a minimum. When considering that the evidence of a good methodology is its deliverables, one must find the balance between too much and not enough documentation.

In some, even many, cases, you will be able to implement with a very light documentation footprint. The problems, however, will become manifest in the future when you need to train a new employee, upgrade your software, or review a business process. It might become difficult to transfer knowledge that is in people's heads, understand why the system was customized a certain way, or recall the rationale behind certain functional decisions.

BUDGET CONTROL

Budget: a mathematical confirmation of your suspicions.

—A. A. Latimer

Key Takeaway: Your budget is one of the three project management elements over which you must assert your authority.

As you manage the scope and schedule of your project, you also need to keep cost control at the forefront of your project activities. All these three levers work in relation to one another and need to be in balance at all times.

No one will argue the benefits of budget control, at least no one who is not swimming in cash. Then again, I'm sure Elon Musk, Bill Gates, or Warren Buffet know what a budget is. Which makes me wonder if the Dubai Police Department understands the concept. Have you seen the outrageous supercars they drive to patrol their city? Go ahead, google it.

Scope

The first obvious way to keep your budget in check is to keep a tight leash on your scope. *(Some people might claptrap and mention something about their spouse and a credit card, but I am not going there without my lawyer present.)* If your scope increases, so will your budget, and most likely your schedule. This may seem simple, but as your project progresses, you will discover new information and some surprises that will add new tasks to your workload.

You might also catch your core team looking to add items to their shopping cart, a normal occurrence as they work to design the best possible system and find themselves highly invested in the endeavor. One of the important missions of your steering committee is to keep the project scope reasonable by prioritizing and strategically pushing change requests to later phases.

In a previous chapter, we talked about handling scope during the planning phase of the project. Handling the scope should be an ongoing, continuous task. When riding a wild horse in a rodeo, you can't lose your focus or lower your attention.

Information Gathering

An important aspect of controlling your budget, one which will greatly improve your performance, is making sure all pertinent data is readily available. If it takes too long to receive and process invoices and time sheets, you will struggle to get a good picture of where you stand at any given moment.

There is a parallel between analyzing your project's financial information and handling accounting duties in your business. If it takes too long to close each month, it becomes difficult to evaluate the financial health of your organization. Your management decisions are slowed, and you become more vulnerable.

Communication

Sharing your budget status with your team on a regular basis promotes due diligence on their part. You empower each team member to make decisions and adopt behaviors that will be favorable to your purse. As Simon Sinek says, "Give authority to those closest to the information."

Lack of communication can be detrimental, as people will assume all is well and they may act like project resources are an open bar. Even when all is well, it is good to emphasize that the budget is not infinite so people remain careful. As they should. *(If some people—*

and it only takes a few—did not abuse the open bar at weddings and events, they wouldn't be handing out tickets for drinks.)

Review and Assess

As you keep an eye on your budget, it is also mandatory to keep an eye on your budget's future regularly. As you track what has been accomplished and what is left on the plate, you will be able to foresee project overruns and catch them in time before they become much more impactful.

By the same token, managing current and future resource usage will help you maximize everyone's time while making sure you don't get caught unaware when additional resources may be needed. The more prepared you are, the more in control you become.

This implies using tools and methods that allow for quick turn-arounds. Examples are shortened billing cycles from your vendors, quick time sheet processing for your employees, and effective accounting and project costing practices.

Case Study

A weekly budget status is a key element of any project my team conducts. This budget statement report is based on our time sheet entries and is useful to our clients to see how much time and money has been spent on their project by us, their partner vendor.

This report compares budgeted hours and dollars against actuals. It also shows what has been invoiced so far. This, however, does not include any other costs that may have been incurred by our clients, such as salaries and licensing. For that reason, comprehensive budget tracking activities should be part of internal project management operations by our customers.

CUSTOMIZING

It's kind of fun to do the impossible.

—Walt Disney

> **Key Takeaway: Customizations can make or break your project.**

Quoting Curt Schilling, "There's not a long track record of people leaving professional sports to become a software developer." This is not what the majority of executives trained for either: all hail Bill Gates! Adapting a solution is definitely one of the most elusive, most difficult to master aspects of ERP implementations. *(Changing something is never easy. Ask my girlfriend. She's been trying to change me for nearly ten years now.)*

Customizations can add tremendous value to your business application: they allow you to tailor your software solution to perfectly meet your requirements. Whatever distinguishes you from your rivals and gives you that competitive edge is what defines you as an organization; it is your personality. If this uniqueness brings with it some specific policies, rules, and tools of the trade, then you can most assuredly demonstrate a viable return on investment and gain much by adapting your ERP solution to these specific processes.

Charlie Kaufman had his character John Laroche say the following in his movie *Adaptation* (not a movie adaptation, but a movie called *Adaptation*): "Adaptation is a profound process. Means you figure out how to thrive in the world." Max McKeown writes, "Adaptability is about the powerful difference between adapting to cope and adapting to win."

Likewise, should you decide to modify your ERP system, you must do it to win…something. Modifying your system can be a very risky proposal, and therefore, it must be totally justifiable.

The risk in customizing your software comes from various elements inherently attached to the endeavor, such as modifying code written by someone else, modifying code that can be very complex, or changing a program behavior without fully understanding all the ramifications. When facing complex and difficult modifications, we should always expect the unexpected. As Lauren Fleshman puts it, "Perfect preparation doesn't exist. Excellent adaptation does."

Evaluating and scoping a customization can be tricky. The complexity of any customization is inversely proportionate to our ability to evaluate the effort required to complete it. This is one of the key reasons why ERP implementations get financially blown out of proportion and fail to be delivered on time.

That being said, once you have established the necessity to customize your system, there exist various ways to mitigate the risk and improve your level of control. Relying on good methodology and adhering to high development standards will help a great deal. This is an area where the Agile development approach discussed in a previous chapter can also be helpful.

Documentation

A thoroughly astute business case should support each change. The return on investment and the functional ramifications of any customization should be clear. This information needs to be properly documented to support the team effort but also for future reference. Program code should also be judiciously documented and written following the strictest standards.

Testing

Good testing is paramount. Developers will perform unit testing, which consists of testing their code and making sure it performs according to specifications. Their testing is typically limited to the area their code affects.

Business analysts perform functional testing. Functional testing normally encompasses a larger scope as analysts validate the potential ramifications of that change by testing business processes, not just features.

The most important part of testing remains to be user acceptance testing. In a traditional ERP deployment, super users own the data and the business processes. Their understanding of business operations, exceptions, and other conditions often surpasses the knowledge of the business analysts, who typically know the system better. With support from business analysts, users should thoroughly test the changes to certify they perform as intended.

Despite all this thoroughness and required diligence, and even after a specific modification gets approved and promoted to your production environment, it is not abnormal to find bugs. Edsger W. Dijkstra is famous in the technological world for (among other contributions) saying that "testing shows the presence, not the absence, of bugs." A stabilization period in which further problems can be unearthed always ensues, as thousands upon thousands of lines of code get executed each day while users operate the application.

Upgrading

From time to time, software companies release new versions of their software. There are often multiple benefits to keeping up to date with the latest and newest: continued support, new features, new technologies, etc. Despite these benefits, companies often hesitate to migrate. One of the major deterrents to following a proposed migration path by a software vendor is often the fear of migrating custom code. Complex customizations needing to be merged with new code can increase the cost of a migration process as well as the risk of having something break.

This is a very real challenge, and it should be considered when evaluating the benefits of customizations. Depending on the application and its underlying technology, it is sometimes possible to adapt and code without extensive intrusion into the existing programs.

Case Study

Customizations can be mission-critical in some instances. Some of my customers have invested significant amounts of money in customizing their ERP solution and/or integrating it with in-house applications.

One customer integrated their specific, custom shop floor manufacturing application into their ERP. Their manufacturing application was a perfect fit for their unique industrial operations, and it made more sense to keep it than replace it with standard ERP functionality.

Another customer had us develop an invoicing engine able to process hundreds of thousands of transactions daily, retrieving this data from another system and generating invoices within the ERP application.

In both cases, the final solution became a strategic differentiator and helped to reinforce the client's uniqueness within a very competitive market. Despite the expense, it was still worth the effort.

A word concerning customizations and software upgrades. With their push to the cloud using Dynamics 365 Business Central, Microsoft has introduced extensions. Extensions support customizations that do not invade native programming. The Microsoft code remains intact as these extensions run within Business Central through hooks in the code called subscribers.

Think of it as a service road onto which you can ride, exiting from the highway. Getting back on the highway exactly where you were when you exited happens once you've traveled the length of the service road. Nope, it's not time travel! Excel plug-ins are a form of extension.

The extensions make future upgrades easier as there is no need to compare and merge code anymore.

CHANGE MANAGEMENT

Intelligence is the ability to adapt to change.

—Stephen Hawking

> **Key Takeaway: Embracing change will help you grow, but managing change will help you grow straight.**

Change is inevitable. "Change before you have to," says Jack Welch. As we discussed in a previous chapter, you will most likely be forced to replace your business application at some point due to compelling external pressures.

I would like to share with you a very interesting position maintained by Eric B. Dent and Susan Galloway Goldberg, as they challenge the myth that employees resist change and that management must overcome that resistance. They contend that although people may resist loss of status, pay, or comfort, they do not specifically resist change but simply do not embrace it. The nuance here is significant.

Financial concerns aside, I have yet to meet someone who has resisted changing her rickety old car for a brand-new one. Changing cars is a fun thing to do. *(Now, please do not tell me about your friend who will not let go of his very, very old T-shirt. That doesn't count as it invalidates my example.)*

The point I am trying to make is that change is not a poison that employees viscerally fear. Change can truly be good if there are clear benefits for them.

As an executive, you experience your own fears when considering the purchase of an ERP system, but are you really afraid of changing systems? Could it be that you are more concerned with loss of control or perhaps fear of failure?

Jeffrey M. Hiatt, in his book *ADKAR—A Model for Change in Business, Government and Our Community*, explains, "A common mistake made by many business leaders is to assume that by building awareness of the need for change, they have also created desire."

Allowing your employees to be involved in the change process and making decisions from the very beginning, to understand why it must happen, to grow with it as you have, and to truly be a part of it, will greatly improve your chance of success.

However, when you can rally your employees to your cause by making it their cause as well, you are not fighting with them through the change anymore; you just found yourself a team of ambassadors to make it happen. Participation and communication are probably the most important elements to consider when managing change.

Imagine climbing Mount Everest for the first time. You are part of a group of first-time climbers, and along with your fellow adventurers, you feel excited but also quite nervous about the challenge that lies ahead of you.

Your guide and his team of experienced climbers have explained to you what will happen during the climb: where you will stop to rest, what equipment you will use and how it works, which protocols and safety measures will be followed, how your body will react to the lack of oxygen and the cold as you go higher and higher. All these minute details can mean the difference between life and death.

Now imagine that they did not. Would you still feel excited or perhaps a tad more nervous? How about a good dose of cortisol, adrenaline, and glucose? Those are the chemicals that your system produces when you are afraid. Many of your employees may feel this way if you tackle an ERP deployment while keeping them in the dark.

Moreover, despite having been prepared, you are going to go through ups and downs as you face challenges during the climb. This is also typical in ERP implementations and when dealing with change.

Activities, methods, and protocols used in change management ensure that your organization is ready for the change by preparing and supporting each individual and team to successfully achieve your project objectives.

Change management sometimes gets confused with project management. While project management deals with budget, scope, scheduling, and the execution of activities to achieve the stated goals, you could say that change management deals with the people executing these activities.

John F. Kennedy said, "Change is the law of life, and those who look only to the past or present are certain to miss the future."

The ultimate goal of change management is to turn people's heads and have them look toward the future.

Case Study

I remember attending a trade show where a business owner approached me to discuss an ERP deployment. He fully understood the need for a new ERP system. His Excel spreadsheet nightmare was about to turn into a corporate obituary.

What was his main concern? What was he insisting on? Managing costs. More precisely, he was making sure his project would not turn out to be four times as expensive as the original estimate, just like it was for his friend—owner of company XYZ—who, by the way, still does not have a working application to show for his efforts.

Losing money is obviously a big deal. But in there, peeling the layers of this onion, we also find loss of control, fear of failure, and perhaps even loss of status.

MOTIVATION

Peel back the facade of rigorous methodology
projects and ask why the project was successful,
and the answer is people.

—Jim Highsmith

> **Key Takeaway: Motivation is primarily an internal-
> ized and self-guided process.**

Have you ever tried motivating your teenager or young adult to
clean up after themselves? Have you been successful? Yes? What
torture mechanism did the trick for you? Please share it with me—I
certainly need the help.

We often believe that people can be motivated by external stimuli:
sometimes positive (such as bonuses, contests, and gifts) and
other times negative (such as penalties, financial or otherwise).
Some think that negative external stimuli, such as fear of losing
your job, can motivate employees.

It is true that, to a certain extent, external stimuli can work. You will
find, however—and this is supported by research—that its effects
are temporary and the need to create greater and greater stimuli
can tax your creativity to its limit.

Susan Fowler explains in her book *Why Motivating People
Doesn't Work...and What Does* that contrary to popular belief, your
employees are always motivated; the key factor is not to motivate
them but to understand what level of motivation they have achieved
and how to help and guide them toward elevating their motivation
to a level that is more conducive to achievement and fulfillment.

Fowler identifies the following six motivational outlooks:

1. **Disinterested**. This outlook can almost be associated with a total lack of motivation. The individual feels disconnected, and the activity he is involved in seems like a waste of time. A high school student sitting in a history class comes to mind.

2. **External**. The individual in this state of mind finds benefit in the activity, but those benefits are external, such as an opportunity to exert power or take advantage of the situation for personal gain. A salesperson attending a useless meeting in which he will be recognized as the top seller in the company, thereby enhancing his status, may be a good example.

3. **Imposed**. Falling in line is the obvious by-product of this outlook. The person performing this activity does it because everyone else is doing it and wishes to avoid the repercussions of not being involved. Think of that teenager we mentioned earlier and a family on a cleaning sprint on a beautiful Saturday morning. We're not talking about the student throwing paper clips at her history teacher, but mine, who needs to learn to clean up. And what is it with teenagers?

These first three outlooks are qualified as suboptimal. Despite marking a progression from 1 to 3 in the ability of the individual to self-regulate and better fulfill their psychological needs, we are experiencing short-term motivational effects and still have not achieved an optimal motivational outlook, such as these described below:

4. **Aligned**. The activity you are participating in provides a clear benefit, as you are able to link it to a significant value, such as learning. That same history student, now a young adult, is engaged in a college class that is directly linked to their chosen curriculum.

5. **Integrated**. This outlook is very powerful, as you can link the activity to a life or work purpose. I would surmise that Mother Teresa lived most of her life with this particular perspective.

6. **Inherent**. The inherent outlook comes from your positive feelings toward the activity. Playing a round of golf or running may be examples of activities that are conducive to the inherent motivational outlook. You just like doing this.

Being able to identify one's motivational outlook, or that of an employee or coworker, is the first step in being empowered to positively influence said outlook. It requires skills that can be honed, developed, and improved.

Moreover, as just mentioned, the last three outlooks are better at empowering an individual to self-regulate and better fulfill their psychological needs. But what psychological needs are we talking about? The self-determination theory outlines three important elements that allow people to grow psychologically. They are autonomy, competence, and connection.

This understanding of motivational behavior supports involving your people early in the change process, as stated in the previous chapter, as it greatly improves the probability of having their goals align with those of the organization. This would increase their feeling of autonomy, of them being in control of their objectives, even though they might be shared. It would also increase their motivation by being able to make a difference: having a significant impact on the outcome of the project.

Competence for your general employees will be addressed when they are able to learn new skills and shown that they can work with the new system. If you communicate with them often and keep them in the loop as the implementation progresses, their insecurity might diminish, and their sentiment of competence should increase.

Your super users, your core team, will go through the same process, but in their case, another factor plays an important part. They must have enough confidence in the project's success to keep that feeling of competence ever present. They must be provided with all the resources they need to ensure their triumph over the many challenges they will face during the ERP rollout.

Finally, connection is all about teamwork and belonging. If you create and promote a strong positive culture within the company but also within the project team, you will be promoting relatedness.

I also believe that being able to positively impact your employees' motivation requires a certain level of sensitivity that is based on the value that one perceives in these same employees. As Jim Goodnight puts it: "Treat employees like they make a difference, and they will." If we take a quick break and go back to read the quote at the top of this chapter again, and then agree that our people are our most important asset, then Goodnight's quote becomes exceedingly significant.

I recently read a book written by Gary Chapman called *The 5 Love Languages*. In his book, he explains how people respond differently to acts of service, receiving gifts, quality time, words of affirmation, and physical touch. We all have one or two that stand out. Using these languages is more natural to us, and we respond immediately when people *speak* them to us. The challenge is finding out what the key languages of your spouse or partner are so that you can press the right buttons. *(I am sure my girlfriend speaks all five equally well. Great for me at the receiving end, but a lot of work at the giving end!)*

Okay. So where am I going with this? These five languages can also be used in the workplace as languages of appreciation! Understanding these languages and leveraging these new skills with your employees will also help bolster morale. I recommend the book *The 5 Languages of Appreciation in the Workplace. (Why not read both while you're at it? Nope. I didn't receive any money from Mr. Chapman.)*

Case Study

I recently read a story in 24/7 The First Person You Must Lead Is You, written by Rebecca "Becky" Halstead, about how she, as a commanding officer, took the time to impart upon a young soldier how important his task was to the army he was serving. The young man seemed disheartened to be assigned the duty of preparing helicopter fuel without realizing how mission success and even lives depended on his due diligence. He perked up once he saw things differently.

As a consultant, I have often dealt with insecure employees and doubting team members. I would often emphasize to them how learning and adapting to their new ERP would help them acquire new skills and that they should readily include this information in their resume. These new skills are highly valuable in the workplace. Many of these employees, often super users, found themselves promoted to new positions after the project as their value and contribution to the company had changed for the better during that time.

Without knowing it, I was working on their motivational outlook. Had I known about these motivational concepts at the time, I would have been more proactive in determining the impact of my comments and dispensing such encouragement.

COMMUNICATION

The single biggest problem in communication is the illusion it has taken place.

—George Bernard Shaw

> **Key Takeaway: Communication is one of the greatest challenges of change management, and if you get it wrong, better to do too much than not enough.**

Project management and change management rely heavily on good communication. Communicating progress, sharing vision, and keeping the organization informed are all key objectives of good communication during a deployment project.

Communication within an organization is not that different from communication between two people: someone has a message to convey and both communicators have a responsibility to make sure that the message is delivered with integrity and fully understood. This implies a bidirectional effort that includes feedback and a continuous process.

I remember visiting the San Diego Zoo and watching two groups of monkeys quarrel and go after each other, rallying their friends to their cause and trying to win their argument and make their point. In this specific situation, it was, "Don't touch the little one." It was fascinating. They seemed effective enough in communicating. Why do we humans have so much difficulty with communication? Could it be that as the most intelligent species on earth, we inject too much nuance and too many gray zones in our process? *(I can at least confirm that I do not read minds. Another piece of trivia coming from my personal experience in love relationships.)*

In fact, after recently attending a course on one-to-one communication, I learned that the main reason is that most of us are not trained to communicate properly and we really have no clue what we are doing. Communicating effectively involves skills and techniques that can be learned.

A good communication plan must be part of your change management process. That plan has to allow frequent communications via multiple channels, making sure all can be reached, wherever they are. These channels also include one-on-one conversations with employees and project members. Having your management team spend time to share the vision and objectives of the project with your people can be invaluable in fostering the proper motivational outlooks, as we covered in the last chapter.

Another benefit of communicating on a personal level, not just through media, is that it greatly enhances the feedback loop that must be present to ensure that the message properly addresses employee concerns and issues. Communication is a two-way street.

Complete disclosure is also highly recommended for effective communication: clearly communicate the objectives and mission of the project, communicate new information as soon as it becomes available and before it becomes rumor, and make sure that all communications are accurate and exact, thus avoiding any potential loss of credibility. This should also include disclosing pitfalls, mistakes, and challenges.

There's no shame in looking for help to improve your personal or corporate communication abilities.

Let me close this with words from James Humes: "The art of communication is the language of leadership."

Case Study

A true story heard from a peer:

In preparation for their ERP project, employees of I Forgot Who They Were LLC spent countless hours printing all their data to prevent loss of information during the implementation.

This happened at the beginning of this century, but it still serves as a good reminder that, technical considerations aside, insecurities were prevalent in that situation and a lack of information proved to be highly counterproductive.

SECTION 5

DELIVERY

TRAINING

Tell me and I forget, teach me and I may remember, involve me and I learn.

—Benjamin Franklin

> **Key Takeaway: Any tool placed in untrained hands can be dangerous.**

You may have selected and designed the best system, involving the best consultants the world has ever known, but if your people cannot use it effectively, your organization is a Formula 1 race car stuck in the pits.

Training is a very important task, which should not be taken lightly. You keep hearing this in every chapter, but that is the nature of an ERP implementation: it is a series of pivotal steps that need to be performed effectively to ensure success.

Very often, the issue with training is that it is underestimated. As Steven Scott Phillips puts regarding the "train the trainer" approach, "It is not realistic to assume someone can be trained several weeks before go-live and expect him/her to deliver quality training."

If you rely on that approach, your super users should be involved from the very beginning and master the application by the time they have the responsibility of training your regular users. This is what we promote in our projects. Your super users also need to rely on well-written user guides and a thoroughly tested and working application.

If at the end of your project your vendor would be open to hiring some of your super users, then you've done your job right. This means they can really become your front liners, your go-to people.

When super users feel overwhelmed with the necessary learning curve, I often tell them that they can suffer now or suffer even more later. I say this with compassion, but it does carry the important message that learning new stuff is hard but necessary. Because it is hard, some people refuse to embrace change, but your super users have an important responsibility as ambassadors of your new ERP.

The rest of your people should be trained on what they need to know to accomplish their job, but they should also be informed of the impact of their work on the rest of the organization. Using an ERP system means integrating the various functions and processes of the business, which also means that each department is now dependent upon others and vice versa. Each link forming the chain becomes significant in maintaining the chain's integrity, and as an organization, you're only as strong as your weakest link.

As you train your users in preparation for the upcoming go-live, make sure that you validate their understanding of the new procedures and how to properly use the system. Things may look peachy until you go live and find out folks are not that ready after all. You don't have to conduct formal exams and add to the already mounting stress, but making sure everyone is comfortable and proficient enough should not be left to chance.

Your system is more than servers, programs, and a database. It also comprises your people, and they must take ownership of the data and business processes, as we've previously mentioned. *(I like harping this repeatedly.)* As Raymond L. Manganelli and Mark M. Klein wrote, "Good people can make a bad system work; bad people cannot make a good system work."

Case Study

The timing of your training is important. If you train your end users too early, they will forget much of what they learned by the time they get to use the system, but if you train them too late, they will not have time to properly absorb the new knowledge. This is why involving super users at the very beginning of the project and insisting on the quality of your documentation become so important.

You know how the saying goes: "Make it idiotproof, and someone will just make a better idiot." This cynical statement does not imply your people are stupid but emphasizes the importance of properly designing and testing systems. It also points out how users can be creative in finding new ways to utilize the system, thus further promoting the value of proper training.

In one particular implementation, I recall having to stop the project after finishing our piloting sessions—you know, integrated testing. The company had a major business issue, something like activating another warehouse or having to repair the CEO's private jet.

They paused the project for nearly two months, and when we returned, we had to retrain the super users. They had not kept their knowledge fresh by staying in the system and practicing regularly. This will not surprise anyone. This anecdote further enhances the importance of timing and momentum.

GOING LIVE

A task is not done until it is done.

—Louis Fried

Key Takeaway: Evaluate your risk, and plan every step as if you were launching a space shuttle.

Going live is the milestone you have worked so hard to achieve. It is the key turning point, and often, there is no going back. A difficult go-live filled with problems and delays can leave a bad impression on your people and prove costly to your organization. *(Bring out the Tylenol!)*

You want to make sure that flipping the switch is a smooth and effective transition. Oh yes, often complex and delicate, but it can still be smooth and effective, like a precisely executed surgery. *(Except in this case, nobody is blissfully put under—we are all very much aware of what is going on.)*

To achieve a smooth go-live, you must first be ready. Meticulously prepared. If you fail to properly assess your readiness, and by extension your risk, then you will most likely experience a difficult flip of the switch. This can be a real turnoff. Marianna Bradford writes: "Remember that if you fail to implement, who cares what the software [ERP] does?"

Good project management helps in risk assessment. Properly completing and closing each task ensures that the deliverables are what they should be and that no stone remains unturned: your business system must be ready, and that includes both software and people. Identify any weak areas, and prepare contingency plans should issues crop up during go-live. Create scenarios and identify ways you can circumvent problems, real or otherwise. Determine when it is still possible to abort the operation if a major crisis occurs.

It is good practice to rely on a detailed checklist for go-live, which should include all chronological tasks needed to be performed for a smooth and efficacious go-live, technical or otherwise. For each task, identify prerequisites, responsible individuals, and deadlines. Make sure this list is distributed to all partners and colleagues involved or impacted by the activation of the new system and that all key personnel can be contacted should the need arise. This is where the work performed during your pilot testing can be very helpful as it should be mostly a repeat of what was done back then. *(You may need to find out which nearby restaurants are open for [late] deliveries. This time, we recommend sushi, as it is easier to digest.)*

Case Study

The first ERP deployment I witnessed was a project conducted by my former employer. We're traveling back in time to the mid-nineties. ERP deployments were more challenging back then as the technology was not what it is today.

I left the organization before the go-live date but remained in touch with the people there. It was a difficult project from the beginning, missing the required leadership from top management, with each department head pulling for their own department and sometimes even sabotaging the project. The level of indifference, or plain resistance, was nearly unbelievable.

With the added pressure of meeting deadlines, the project team ended up making the decision to go live and wrap up this project from hell without being fully ready. Did they lose too many players along the way? Was the risk assessment faulty? Were people just looking for some closure? Regardless, after going live, the company ran into multiple problems and was not able to ship goods for many days.

APPLICATION LIFE CYCLE

Software is a great combination between artistry
and engineering.

—Bill Gates

**Key Takeaway: Grass should be cut, engines
must be oiled, and software systems have to be
maintained.**

After going live, you will transition to support. This process may
be more or less complicated, depending on your vendor, but
essentially, all project tasks are completed, approved, and closed.
You are now using the system continuously and as intended...or
are you?

Despite all the hard work that went into it, you might have missed
something and bugs might still exist. There is no better testing than
real life, when all your users are in the application daily, finding
new ways to break it, intentionally or not. It's almost impossible to
test and prepare for all possible contingencies and with the same
volume of transactions as when the application is in production.

No worries—a stabilization period of three to six months is normal.
People should become comfortable using their new tool, and all
the kinks need to be ironed out. While this process takes place,
you should notice your support needs diminishing as time goes
by, as long as you differentiate between real issues and new
requirements or ideas for improvements. Improving your solution
once people get more acquainted with it is obviously not the same
as fixing problems.

If you identified clear objectives at the start of the project, objectives that can be measured by key performance indicators, then these KPIs can be reviewed during the stabilization period to see if they are met, or even surpassed, as the application becomes more stable and users more competent.

Once you are satisfied that all is well, it may be time to tackle the next phase, if you had planned multiple project phases. You may have intentionally postponed the deployment of some features, or perhaps changes in the organization or in your industry are forcing you to turn them on now, create new reports, or activate new modules. A system is alive and should be maintained accordingly. Again, nothing unusual here.

I would emphasize that your documentation, functional specification documents, user guides, and so on are also part of the system and should also be maintained. Letting them gather dust depletes their usability and their value, and when business processes and procedures only exist in people's heads, your organization is at risk. If you were in this situation before implementing, there's no way you want to go back to that risky state of affairs once again.

Software Upgrades

Managing upgrades is an important topic pertaining to your application's life cycle, and that can prove quite challenging. Vendors will produce new versions—how do you deal with those? When do you upgrade? Is it worth the investment? Help! Please!

There is no recipe for this. The issue has to be treated on a case-by-case basis. Any decision is influenced by various elements, such as the development life cycle of your vendor: how often do they produce a new version, the underlying technology, your customizations, etc.?

Let's try to address some of these elements one by one, keeping in mind that they are all interrelated.

Development Life Cycle

In on-premises environments, the frequency at which your vendor produces new software versions will have an impact on your decision to upgrade or not. What new features are included in each version is also significant. Assuming a yearly version with limited new features that you have not really been waiting for, you may prefer to skip a few years before you upgrade, especially if the process is costly.

Keep in mind, however, that if you wait too long, the version you are using may stop being supported. When that happens, bug fixes are no longer published and support calls are not possible. You must evaluate the potential impact on your organization if you delay upgrading under such circumstances.

Technology

The technology and the application architecture have a notable impact on your decision to upgrade. We discussed extensions in the chapter on customizing. If upgrading involves comparing and merging code, as previously stated, this adds a layer of complexity tied to upgrades, and it is clearly inherited from the technology.

If you deployed in the cloud, there's a good chance your solution will always be the latest version. This is one of the benefits of being on the cloud. It may be upgraded automatically for you. Case closed. This serves both your software editors' interests and yours.

If your software resides on your servers, on-premises, then there must be a process to migrate the data and the code. The database and programming language used to create the application contribute to that process's complexity, which, with its underlying cost, will affect your decision to upgrade or not.

Can you access the data and/or the code? Can you perform the upgrade yourself, internally? Do you need the help of your software partner? Which tools can you rely on? These are all questions that need to be answered before you can commit yourself.

Customizations

One of the most influential elements of your upgrade decision has to do with your customizations. How easily can they be migrated and included in the new version? Are you using extensions?

I have crossed paths with some ERP clients that have become stuck with a version so modified that their vendor could not upgrade it, even if they were the author of the modifications. Let me rephrase that: a software vendor modified their application but was not able to upgrade it later. What? How is that even possible? Well, it has to do with a few factors.

Firstly, consider the technology. Is the application easy to customize? Is the software platform flexible and technologically advanced enough that modifications are less invasive, more peripheral?

Secondly, is your software vendor respecting the data model as the solution evolves, providing backward compatibility? Simply put, are they removing fields and tables in the new version, causing potential migration problems? If so, please see the next point.

Thirdly, are the tools used to migrate the data and merge the customized code powerful enough? This is directly linked to the technology used and the effort deployed by your vendor to provide effective migration tools. It is not a bad idea to ask about this before you buy your solution.

Lastly, were the modifications done using best industry practices? Is the code well documented? Are the changes nonintrusive? Even though customizations can be troublesome and obviously add complexity to an upgrade, it does not mean that customizations are not pertinent and should be avoided at all costs. Customizations should be minimized, but when necessary, they should be done well.

In closing, keeping your system up to date and within the vendor's support window is a good strategic proposition.

PERFORMANCE TUNING

Men are from Mars, women are from Venus,
computers are from hell.

—Jeff Atwood

Key Takeaway: Computers move in mysterious ways. Performance tuning is an elusive and demanding art.

The approach to tuning depends heavily on the infrastructure being deployed, and we will thus discuss both cloud and on-premises technological platforms in this chapter.

Cloud Tuning

If your solution sits in the cloud, the performance issues you might encounter will most likely have to do with your network bandwidth or your Internet connection. Any respectable cloud provider should be actively optimizing performance and tuning their infrastructure. In fact, in a true SaaS deployment, you should not have access to the database and should not be able to tune the application yourself. This narrows down potential problems to the hardware that sits between you and your vendor's cloud infrastructure.

Be aware, however, that some operational deployments may require special hardware configurations and some kind of preprocessing. A good example is rolling out a warehouse management system that uses barcoding equipment, commonly referred to as *Star Trek* tricorders. The volume of inventory transactions generated by such a system may cause performance issues if it communicates directly with your cloud infrastructure. Often, a local server, used to predigest some of that volume before the data is sent to the cloud, may be helpful.

Each case is unique, and mileage may vary. Your networking specialists would work with your software vendor to determine the best hardware combination for you.

On-Premises Tuning

You may be able to perform some stress testing prior to going live, and although this will help in evaluating your system's robustness, it often does not reflect reality like...well, like reality does. Performance problems will often arise after a certain amount of time and may occur for various reasons. You may have increased the number of users over time, turned on some power-hungry features like materials requirement planning, rolled out new customizations or reports that are not optimized for performance, or simply enlarged your database significantly.

Often, an examination of your system may reveal the source of your performance problems: your Windows event log or database management system can provide valuable insight into the issue. On your local system, the most difficult tuning problems to find are often those having to do with either your network infrastructure or your application design. Networking problems require specialists, just like electrical problems require electricians.

Tuning applications is not easy. Most ERP systems are designed in their own proprietary programming language, whose statements are translated to database requests in a structured query language, invisible to the developer. That creates a level of abstraction that makes it more difficult to code efficiently. In most ERP programming languages, you cannot use SQL hints to optimize data retrieval statements.

SQL hints are special command options or strategies that influence how a database will process a data request or instruction. When used properly, it should speed up database access.

(I know this is technical. My recommendation to you, dear reader, if you are indeed a business owner or executive, is to stay away from this stuff. However, mention it in front of your technical team to gain instant respect. You can also try that at your next family reunion to garner unequivocal admiration.)

So how can you improve application performance? Each language has coding best practices that should be followed, but most of the time, effective coding relies on the appropriate use of table indexes. Think of an index as some sort of table of contents for your data: each table in your database contains information and can have multiple indices to help with the retrieval of said information. A good coder understands how database engines retrieve data and can create indices that will speed up the process, especially when dealing with large reports or data-intensive processes.

General Recommendations

As you guessed, performance tuning can be a very technical, geeky topic. If you are still awake, then read on to learn of some basic common sense practices that can help you avoid certain performance problems:

1. Apply your software manufacturer's recommended system requirements.
2. Stay up to date on fixes and corrections published by your software manufacturer. Installing an update may not be mandatory, and there are tactical decisions to be made here. If a corrective update does not impact your company because it doesn't address a feature you are utilizing, maybe you ought not to install it. This could avoid destabilizing your system.

3. If possible, stay current on the most recent software version.

4. Make sure your operating system is up to date with all the latest patches and fixes—especially for security reasons.

5. Isolate your production server. Do not perform development on your production server, database, or service. Not only can that impact performance, but it also puts your company at risk.

6. Monitor your system.

Performance tuning is the topic of significant training classes, but to leave you with a flavorful impression of its technical and capricious nature, let's end with a medley of quotes from Chief Engineer Montgomery Scott of the starship USS *Enterprise*: "I dannae if she can take any more, Captain! This jury-rigging won't last for long. I cannot change the laws of physics, Captain! 'Ave got to have thirty minutes!"

Case Study

We recently needed to investigate a performance issue for one of our customers. Recommendation number 5 above is there for a reason. After taking a look at the server and asking some questions, we found out that their internal programmer was using the production server to develop, which included running reports and performing other processor-intensive tasks. This was how we were able to explain the degradation in performance they had been experiencing of late.

(That's all I have to say. Unless you want to hear about the many times I tuned an Oracle database by altering the buffer cache parameters. No? Didn't think so.)

APPLICATION SECURITY

No one can build their security upon the nobleness of another person.

—Willa Cather

> **Key Takeaway: Security requires meticulous design and thorough testing.**

We quoted this adage in a previous chapter: "Make it idiotproof, and someone will just make a better idiot." We can easily adapt this quote to security by changing one word: "Make it hacker-proof, and someone will just make a better hacker."

Sadly, in today's world, crime is perpetrated, and wars are waged in the virtual universe as much as the physical one. You must absolutely invest money, time, and effort into protecting one of your most precious assets: your data.

Your business application will provide you with the ability to configure security: grant or revoke access to features, screens, data, etc. This functionality can sometimes be very sophisticated. The more sophistication you include in your security strategy, the more time it will require for planning, configuration, and validation. You already know protecting your organization is of paramount importance, so what is the point of shredding tons of paper if anyone can access your data on the computer? Activate the alarm system, lock the door, and swallow the key! Figuratively speaking, of course.

Secure Each Component

With an on-premises installation, the security of each system component must be examined. Your operating system, network, databases, and applications require appropriate protection. In a cloud deployment, some of that security is abstracted and transparent to you, but present nonetheless.

Your information technology administrator is responsible for the security of your infrastructure, but it may not be the case for your business systems. Your ERP system contains sensitive financial and operational information and perhaps personal information about your employees. Good care must be given to protect this valuable data.

As this book is written, many systems now use multifactor authentication (MFA), which requires users to enter more than a password to access an application. Their identification is validated via a second step such as, for example, entering a code received by text message on a phone. This method provides greater security than operating systems (Windows) or application credentials (log-in/password).

Segregate Duties

Another effective method of reducing your risk and increasing your control is to apply segregation rules. Companies who are subjected to the Sarbanes-Oxley Act of 2002 know this form of security measure well.

To reduce the impact of having a user's credentials compromised, procedures are divided into tasks that are assigned to different users. Multiple users are therefore required to complete a particular task, such as paying a vendor. Not only does segregation of duties provide more internal accounting and operational control, but it also improves application security.

Stay Vigilant

Although systems can have flaws and vulnerabilities, the weakest link in cybersecurity is humans. People make mistakes and can be duped. They can forget their key card, share their password, or click on a phishing link, even with the best of intentions. Phishing is the most common hacking technique. Education should, therefore, also be part of your application security strategy.

Implementing a solid security strategy is an iterative and time-consuming process that requires extensive testing. Your security strategy should be in place for your conference room pilot, but do not be surprised if you keep on tweaking it beyond your go-live. People come and go, duties and responsibilities change, and therefore, managing security constitutes a regular maintenance task.

Case Study

Some customers choose to keep their system open and their information accessible. They don't invest much in security. This tends to be true of smaller organizations that often cultivate a more open culture as their key people, those in the know, are few, well-known, and often have been for a long time. Implementing security for these businesses tends to be fairly simple and painless.

Many other organizations need to elevate their level of security due to various obligations and constraints. For those companies, this can be a challenging and important task. It typically involves creating roles and assigning permissions on tables, reports, pages, and other objects. Relying on quality user guides is a huge help to determine which roles users should be given. Testing remains the most time-consuming part of this effort, but putting the data together, often in an Excel spreadsheet to be uploaded, is a monk's work.

I have experienced both situations. One way or another, you should expect continuous maintenance as you go forward, with an amount of effort matching the scope of your solution.

DISASTER RECOVERY

Experience is something you don't get until just after you need it.

—Steven Wright

Key Takeaway: Failing to plan and prepare for disaster recovery is setting yourself up for that interesting experience you do not need.

Planning for disaster recovery is often a neglected task, particularly in small- to medium-sized companies, where resources are limited and people are always so busy. Nonetheless, it must be taken seriously to protect your organization from undue risk. If you can't do it yourself, I suggest you have someone help you.

Wikipedia defines *disaster recovery* as "[it] involves a set of policies, procedures and tools to enable the recovery or continuation of vital technology infrastructure and systems following a natural or human-induced disaster."

Disaster recovery is not a discipline that is part of your ERP domain, but your business applications are components of your pool of IT resources and therefore must be included in your disaster recovery plan (DRP).

A disaster recovery plan addresses the following tough question: what if a meteorite drops on my computer room? *(Or what if my mother-in-law paid me a visit at the office? What if my nephew decided to play Minecraft on my business laptop?)* If you run your entire operation in the cloud, then the question would be, what if a big meteorite drops on my cloud provider's much larger computer room?

Planning for the worst involves policies and procedures, as previously mentioned, but it also involves discipline and practice. Remember those fire alarm drills when you were in school? Your recovery plan will involve similar drills, particularly when you consider how quickly technologies evolve and change. You do not want to compound a disaster with another one when you find out the backup you have been relying on for continuous operation is not compatible with your secondary system anymore.

I would also add that disaster recovery is not limited to handling meteorites: any event that can interrupt or disrupt operations should be part of your plan. Cyberattacks, equipment failures, and natural disasters can all affect your organization and cause great harm. Even seemingly minor and inconsequential events can have unwanted ramifications, as anyone who has experience with software updates can attest.

The advent of cloud computing and infrastructure as a service (IaaS) offers more options for disaster recovery. Some companies managing their own on-premises infrastructure will use the cloud as their backup site, a place where a company can temporarily relocate its operations following a debilitating event such as a breach or disaster. *(Or your mother-in-law's visit.)*

For those fully committed to the cloud, the backup site could be another data center where a copycat of your infrastructure lives, preconfigured, primed (meaning, up to date), and ready to go.

Ideally, you want a warm or hot backup site. A warm site is ready to go but needs your data, restored from your latest backup, for example. A hot site is much more difficult to maintain, but this site already has your data and is ready to be activated. This latter approach would greatly limit your downtime but could be too costly if you're not running an airport or keeping tabs on the space station.

It's now clear that the primary objective of disaster recovery is to eliminate or minimize the downtime caused by critical events and allow the business to continue operating as normally as possible.

Case Study

Earlier in my career, I was called in to help two customers who were in a critical situation. Their operations were paralyzed for numerous days due to technical issues. In both instances, it was a database problem that needed days to fix.

I remember one of them more vividly: an operating system fix was installed by their IT personnel on a clustered SQL Server environment, and they conducted the operation in a way that broke the cluster. A cluster is a computer or software structure that provides redundancy. If one server or database fails, a failover occurs, and the twin machine or database in the cluster takes over.

In plain English, they tried to fix something that wasn't broken and ended up breaking something that was working fine.

I was able to make them operational again, but this whole misadventure was very costly. Their greatest cost came from having to reinstall a new software key, as their software license was linked to their hardware. Since they had interrupted their annual maintenance program with their ERP software vendor, they were forced to either repurchase the software or reinstate their maintenance program...penalties included.

SECTION 6

AUTOMATION

WORKFLOWS

There can be economy only where there is
efficiency.

—Benjamin Disraeli

Key Takeaway: Automate the good, eliminate the bad.

Most modern ERP systems now offer business process automation workflows. This functionality can contribute to significantly improving business processes and procedural execution within the organization. Although a little tedious to set up at first, rolling out automation workflows is a mini project that should be on your bucket list. Collaboration can be greatly improved by using automation workflows.

Some of the processes supported by automation workflows include transaction approvals, report printing and delivery, automatic scanning of purchase invoices using optical character recognition, document-filing requests, notifications sent to key people or groups when certain conditions occur, etc.

If a given business process is well documented, you already know who does what and when. You can now look at areas of the process that can be optimized with (more) technology. We would recommend automating one specific step, testing, and improving it until it operates perfectly. You can concentrate on the subsequent steps, one by one, until the entire process has been optimized. Then move on to another process.

One important thing to keep in mind, however, is that your processes need to work effectively before you can reap the benefits of automation. In the words of Bill Gates, "The first rule of any technology used in a business is that automation applied to an efficient operation will magnify the efficiency. The second is that automation applied to an inefficient operation will magnify the inefficiency."

This statement from Mr. Gates reminds me of James Clear's book called *Atomic Habits*. In his book, James describes the feedback loop behind our habits and provides tools and tricks to help you foster positive habits or reduce bad habits. This serves as a good metaphor for ERP automation. *(Having done both, automating systems and trying to improve or introduce good habits in my life, I can confirm the former being more complex than the latter, but also much easier. Computer systems don't resist change and can be reprogrammed without any argument.)*

Case Study

Tom had just received an email informing him that the credit limit of Plow That Field Inc. had just been increased. As the sales manager, he needed to approve a large order from Plow That Field that had been sitting in his processing queue since that morning. He now knew that Sarah had been made aware of that same order and that she had been able to approve and change their customer's credit limit.

After a couple of clicks, he was satisfied to see the order removed from his list, and he knew an email had been sent to production, allowing them to include this new order in their production plan. Confident that their customer would receive their goods on time, he was also quite happy to see that he would be punctual in meeting his friend John for lunch.

This typical scenario illustrates how automation can improve your employees' lives and how you can accomplish more with the same number of people. Setting up automations can be time-consuming and can even occasionally require customizations, but the benefits can be immense. Applying Pareto law makes sense: 20 percent of your processes, once automated, should provide 80 percent of the benefits.

Another example, real this time, is a customer using OCR to process payables invoices. If your vendor invoices are recurring—meaning most of your vendor invoices are being received repeatedly and regularly—you can configure OCR templates using a partner solution on Business Central to scan PDF invoices automatically and have them created in the application without anyone keying in any data.

WAREHOUSE MANAGEMENT SYSTEMS

Trade isn't about goods. Trade is about information. Goods sit in the warehouse until information moves them.

—C. J. Cherryh

Key Takeaway: A WMS is another module that provides efficiency gains and improves the overall operation of your business.

Implementing a warehouse management system (WMS) can greatly improve both the efficiency of your warehouse personnel and the precision of your inventory. With the proper discipline and tools, it becomes easier to receive and locate goods, move them around, ship them, or count them.

Sometimes introducing a simple warehouse management system with a few barcode readers (which, as you may remember, I like to call *Star Trek* tricorders) is enough to reap tremendous rewards.

In the previous chapter, we discussed workflow automation. A WMS is an automation tool. Other than improved efficiencies, some of the most important benefits of introducing such a system in your organization include reduced operational costs, improved inventory accuracy, and maximum space utilization.

Real-time and accurate inventories will, in turn, provide higher-quality inputs into your production planning cycle, make procurement more efficient, and increase customer satisfaction.

You should also notice a decrease in receiving and shipping errors, since typing entries will be avoided by scanning bar codes.

As is often the case, deploying a WMS can be identified as a subsequent phase of your global ERP road map, a key element of your continuous improvement strategy.

Below are the most common supported features you would find in a WMS:

Picking

Picking for sales or production orders supports various methods such as order picking, batch picking, wave picking, etc.

Order picking is a simple way of picking all the products you need to fulfill a given order.

Batch picking involves aggregating picking requirements together—for example, a list of orders—so that you only go down the aisles once to get all the required goods. This is obviously more efficient than picking one order at a time.

Wave picking will be used in high-volume warehouses when batch picking still creates too much traffic. With wave picking, the aggregated orders are sorted by zone so that pickers can work in their respective areas without bumping into each other.

Receiving

Receiving is often accomplished in a receiving zone where you will later break down the pallets and move the goods to their appropriate inventory locations. Directed put-away is when the system suggests where to place your stock. This is achieved by implementing a set of rules or algorithms that your WMS will rely on. I can see this area being further improved with artificial intelligence.

Counting

WMS supports various counting methods, such as the common physical count, but also cycle counts and spot counts.

A full physical count, normally performed once a year, consists of thoroughly counting every item in stock, going through every nook and cranny.

Cycle counts consist of regularly counting goods based on their value or velocity. The velocity of inventory represents how frequently they are manipulated. The higher the value and velocity, the higher the frequency of counts. When cycle counting is well established and mastered within a warehouse, it can eliminate the necessity of performing physical counts as it greatly enhances ongoing inventory accuracy.

Spot counts, sometimes called ad hoc counts, will occur when you suspect an issue with a particular item, bin location, or rack. It could be that someone reported missing inventory that should be there. Perhaps you know errors were made in that area and you need to be sure of what you have. The unplanned counts can be very useful in maintaining the integrity of your information.

Palletizing

Palletizing, sometimes called license plating, allows items or lots to be grouped together on a new inventory unit called a license plate number. It then becomes easier to move that unit around, and the system keeps track of every item and/or lot that is part of this pallet. This obviously implies that pallets can also be split and broken down as necessary.

Palletizing can be used in FDA-qualified manufacturing plants, such as food and beverages or pharmaceutical plants. These plants typically rely on batch-process manufacturing. All required raw materials are picked and palletized together before being moved into production as a single or small group of units: the batch.

Palletizing can also be useful in shipping, combining all items from one or multiple sales orders by the same customer on a single pallet.

Stock Locator

A WMS will evidently allow you to track inventory in your warehouse and find a particular item, pallet, lot, or serial number in its bin location, saving your workers a ton of time as they do not have to walk up and down the aisles to find stock.

Case Study

Deploying a WMS can represent a significant effort. For one of my customers who had selected a WMS that was not part of their ERP solution, it meant integrating both systems to ensure real-time inventory was turned into a reality. Implementing a WMS often means reorganizing the warehouse layout, deploying infrastructure, and assigning barcodes to bins and products. Moreover, in most situations, customers take the opportunity to reengineer their warehouse processes.

Such a highly disruptive endeavor will make things worse before they get better. Your employees will have to learn new methods, new tools, and even how to get around in a transformed warehouse.

INTERFACING SYSTEMS

Synergy—the bonus that is achieved when things
work together harmoniously.

—Mark Twain

**Key Takeaway: Building an interface is a delicate
endeavor, but it can streamline your business
processes tremendously.**

Building an interface, a bridge, between two systems can often
be complex and daunting. Most times the systems are designed
around different data models, and the data they need to share must
be understood by both applications. Validating that data before it
travels from one system to the next is as important as validating it
when it is received. *(Having two people communicating to create
a strong, lasting relationship is a nice allegory for this process.)*

Naturally, the more complex the transactions that need to be
supported by an interface, the more delicate and time-consuming
its construction will be.

The good news, however, is that technology makes it easier
for disparate systems to communicate with one another. Most
applications can now exchange extensible markup language (XML)
files, a file format that was created to describe data. Think of it as a
protocol that helps in exchanging information but is much simpler
than electronic data interchange (EDI).

Even better, most ERP systems today contain—or even allow you
to develop—web services. A web service is a form of application
programming interface (API). Web services provide protocols that

support the exchange of data between applications. These types of API can be seen as functions or methods that can be called from external software over Internet communication protocols.

Therefore, an interface or connector built around web services does not involve sending files between applications, instead leveraging the Internet to trade information if the connector knows how to regulate these communications.

(Blah, blah, blah...blah, blah, bleh...)

This topic is somewhat technical, but let's summarize the last two paragraphs: you can now tighten up this thingamajig using a Phillips screwdriver instead of a hard-to-find Security Torx (*google it!*).

Think of it this way: trading files between systems is like sending an email to a friend and waiting for him to receive the email, read it, and reply to you. Using web services to communicate is akin to you picking up the phone, calling your friend, and speaking to him immediately in real time, provided you know what number to dial.

Automatically retrieving the latest exchange rate from Oanda.com every day at 7:00 p.m. can be achieved without human interaction using the proper API. This API is offered by the OANDA website, and if you know how to demand this information using the proper syntax, you can program this data exchange.

Interfacing two different systems is another form of automation, often in separate locations. As more and more solutions are offered on the cloud, the need for (and use of) APIs grows exponentially.

In the end, if you must integrate two systems, keep in mind that doing so requires very thorough testing and can be quite challenging work, but once completed, it can be very rewarding for the organization by eliminating non-value-added work and redundant entries.

Case Study

One of our customers had developed a custom appli-cation to manage their shop floor operations. The shop floor workers were trained on it and comfortable with it, and it fit the process like the proverbial (~~customs agent~~) surgical glove.

It was decided that instead of adapting their new ERP system to mimic the same user experience, an interface would instead be built between both systems.

This interface would allow the shop floor program to read the information it required to function, such as parts data and production orders, while sending the ERP system the results of consumptions, production outputs, and quality testing.

The benefits were improved data integrity and making use of the ERP capabilities in terms of inventory management, costing, and accounting while preserving efficacy in the plant.

ELECTRONIC DATA INTERCHANGE

The shoemaker makes a good shoe because he
makes nothing else.

—Ralph Waldo Emerson

Key Takeaway: EDI is a particular field of expertise within the ERP world, and it often involves partnerships.

Electronic data interchange refers to standard electronic formats business partners use to send orders and receive stock. It is a set of protocols that have been around since the 1960s and are used to exchange information between systems. We are presenting this technology in its own chapter because it differs from the other forms of interfaces discussed in the previous chapter.

Large retailers like Walmart or the automotive industry have been using EDI for many years. You may have to become compliant with the EDI protocol if you trade with those types of organizations. More and more industries are making use of EDI technology, and it seems to be growing in popularity.

EDI allows you to save time and money by automating repetitive tasks, such as sending purchase orders and receiving invoices from vendors. Each type of exchange is supported by a protocol. For instance, invoicing is covered by the EDI 810 transaction code while sending a purchase order requires code 850.

There are dozens of transaction codes that are meant to standardize data exchanges between business partners, and many codes are industry specific. Given the expertise needed to properly support

EDI, ERP vendors will often team up with EDI specialists to offer their customers this functionality. *(Thankfully, I have successfully managed to stay away from this technology for much of my career. I have programmed interfaces and modified two ERP systems for nearly twenty years, but I did not want to get anywhere near this supposed standard that always seemed to require adaptations. Maybe it's just me, but working with EDI always seemed so daunting.)*

EDI modules can be part of the ERP solution you are purchasing, or they can be an external application that uses a connector to communicate with your ERP. Cloud EDI solutions are also gaining popularity.

Case Study

One of our customers deals with Amazon. Like most of our customers, they chose Business Central as their ERP solution. This functionality is not native to Business Central.

They could have selected a module supplied by a specialized EDI partner within the Dynamics 365 ecosystem. Handling multiple trading partners and numerous transaction codes can quickly become a nightmare.

However, considering they only had to support one EDI document and one trading partner, we ended up programming a custom interface for them. (I say we, but no, not me!) This approach proved less costly and as effective.

SECTION 7

MANUFACTURING CONSIDERATIONS

PROCESS VS. DISCRETE MANUFACTURING

The world is content with words, few think of searching into the nature of things.

—Blaise Pascal

Key Takeaway: Overlooking key manufacturing concepts can lead to huge functional impacts.

There are multiple types of manufacturing processes:

1. **Repetitive manufacturing** consists of fabricating goods in rapid succession, usually on some assembly line and often involving automation.
2. **Discrete manufacturing** produces a distinct, identifiable item.
3. **Job shop manufacturing** involves independent tools and machines that can perform various tasks to create a product. It is often used in custom fabrication.
4. **Process manufacturing** can be continuous or in batch mode. A product is made by combining ingredients using a recipe.

To simplify our discussion, we will group repetitive and job shop manufacturing under the discrete manufacturing umbrella as they all produce a distinct, identifiable item.

As we have discussed in the previous chapter, ERP solutions are becoming more specialized. This evolution, I believe, also leads to salespeople and customers who are better prepared and more knowledgeable when it comes to manufacturing solutions. Some years ago, you could frequently find various vendors going after a process manufacturing company with discrete manufacturing solutions ...and win the contract! Nowadays, I still bump into people, sometimes prospects, who are not familiar with the differences between discrete and process manufacturing, but not as regularly as I used to. *(Not because they all bought my book, I assure you.)*

Let us now discuss the differentiating elements of each manufacturing approach and how they translate into ERP application features.

Recipes and BOMs

Process manufacturing is mostly about making products following a transformative process; this is why process manufacturing software will include recipe-based formulation. We are making cookies, medical pills, syrup, paint, shampoo, particle boards, etc. Think of a recipe-based formulation as a cookbook recipe. Ingredients are listed, of course, but also machine and labor requirements, manufacturing instructions, and often quality-testing requirements.

A typical recipe could be structured as follows:

Type	Description	Quantity	Unit of Measure
Input	Material A	10	KG
Input	Material B	5	KG
Input	Material C	.25	G
Machine	Mixer	1	H
Labor	Mixing Technician	1	H
Miscellaneous	Electricity	.01	Per H

Output	Finished Product	12	KG
Manufacturing Instructions			
Quality Instructions			

A complete manufacturing process may involve multiple recipes or manufacturing steps. Formulas are often part of a recipe to help support situations where, for example, the strength of an active ingredient may vary from lot to lot, influencing the quantity required for the mix.

In food processing, reverse bills of materials are often utilized: a single ingredient is fed into the process to produce various outputs or coproducts. Meat cutting is a good example.

Conversely, in discrete manufacturing, we need routers and bills of material to support our operations because we are usually assembling components together to create our product. Examples of discrete manufacturing products are bicycles, heavy machinery, and furniture.

The bill of materials will be a separate entity from the router, but they will be related.

Bill of Materials for Part X		
Item	**Quantity**	**Unit of Measure**
Component A	10	EA
Component B	5	EA
Component C	1	SQFT

Router for Part X		
Work Center/ Machine Center	**Run-Rate**	**Unit of Measure**
Assembly Shop	10	EA

CNC Machine	5	EA
Paint shop	1	HR

It is important to note that you may often find both manufacturing methods in the same organization, more often than not in discrete manufacturing shops. The paint shop in the above example is more akin to process manufacturing than discrete.

Units of Measure

In discrete manufacturing, your result is a single product. A unit—a bike, a chair, a gizmo. Even though you can occasionally package them together, this is routinely the case in process manufacturing. You generally get bulk that will be packaged in various ways. A liquid will be bottled or stored in a tote. If bottled, you will get different bottle sizes and/or different cases: six-pack, twelve-pack, twenty-four-pack. *(Nope! Not thinking about beer.)*

Handling units of measure in a process manufacturing environment is therefore more intricate as you tend to handle bulk quantities of materials that are not easily measured in units. You will be manipulating containers of some liquid that can be counted in drums but also in liters. The conversion from one unit of measure to the other is usually trickier, but on top of that, the measuring of your quantity is definitely more challenging. By opposition, a case of twelve doohickeys is a simple conversion as each component is a single unit.

Another interesting challenge found in process manufacturing is called catch-weight units of measure. We encounter this requirement quite frequently in food processing, as you will be handling units of ingredients that vary in weight. Chickens come to mind. One day, you may get one hundred pounds of meat from twelve chickens, but the next day, you only need eleven chickens to get that same weight.

Quality Control

While quality assurance focuses on preventing quality issues during manufacturing, quality control is focused on measuring product quality. It is part of any manufacturing operation, but the nature of the production process will dictate the kind of quality control that is required.

In process manufacturing, quality control is often performed during the entire fabrication process. This is called in-process testing. Samples are taken at each step, for example, while the meat is curing, the parts are being molded, or the pills are being compressed. Quality tests will also often relate to the machinery that is being used at the time, such as measuring temperature.

In process manufacturing, the impact of a failed quality test can occasionally involve more steps and controls. Produced goods may be stored in quarantine or quality control status pending more testing or reworks.

Even though the same can be said of discrete manufacturing, quality testing is typically sufficient if performed on the assembled product or subcomponents, whether they are made or purchased. Quality control on a chair should be simpler than quality control on Viagra™.

By-Products

Dealing with losses is common in both manufacturing approaches, but by-products and coproducts are more frequent in process manufacturing. They have a value, absorb part of your cost, and can often be used in other products.

When making curd cheese, you get whey. When molding plastic, you will get flashes or rejected parts that can go to regrind and be reused.

Lot Traceability

Although batch manufacturing can occur in both environments, it is more common in process manufacturing, and lot traceability is thus a crucial requirement. Companies that manufacture food and beverages, medication, or chemical products are subjected to stringent manufacturing rules and regulations. These rules are typically enforced by Health Canada or in the United States by the Food and Drug Administration.

Lot traceability, or serial numbering, are features that help companies deal with potential quality issues. Soup, cars, or medication can all be recalled for safety reasons, and a manufacturer's system should support this unlikely but possible—God forbid!—process.

Expiry

As a general rule, discrete products do not expire. They might become scrap metal one day, but they do not make a habit of turning sour overnight. This is the realm of process manufacturing, where ingredients and manufactured goods are often subjected to expiry dates and avoiding losses and ensuring high quality becomes more challenging.

Case Study

I remember helping a customer who had acquired a discrete manufacturing solution a few years before our professional relationship was established. This customer produced hardwood floors, and they had a hard time dealing with coproducts. Whenever they planned to produce three-and-quarter-inch planks, they would also expect two-and-a-half planks, one-and-a-half planks, and so on. They had a planning challenge, and they were working outside their ERP system, using other tools. The stumbling block came from the system's inability to plan coproducts since a BOM could only be linked to one produced item. In other words, a bill of material could not produce two or three items like a process manufacturing recipe would allow.

Whenever they created a production order to make the three-and-quarter-inch planks, they had to create other production orders for the different widths. These production orders, however, had no relationship between them, and their outputs were the result of a single process, not multiple ones.

This is a perfect example of using a discrete manufacturing ERP solution to handle process manufacturing. We did find a way, but it required customizations.

PRODUCTION PLANNING CHALLENGES

Planning is bringing the future into the present so
you can do something about it now.

—Alan Lakein

> **Key Takeaway: Do not rely on a salesperson to do
> production planning: they will break their teeth
> against that task and not have a single tooth left
> in their mouth halfway through the process.**

I know. *(How insensitive of me!)* Before anyone gets offended, I will explain the above takeaway. We hire salespeople because of their ability to talk to people and thrive in the midst of chaos and because they are independent. This is not the type of person you want generating your production plan.

The individual or group you want managing your production plan has to be knowledgeable about both your manufacturing process and your products, of course, but they also have to be very analytical, structured, and disciplined. *(Picky, picky, picky.)* A person who never knew they should have been an accountant or computer programmer can make a good production planner.

The master production schedule will typically plan production backward from the due dates of your sales orders or inventory replenishment orders.

This plan is normally fed to the materials requirement planning engine so it can produce a procurement plan based on order quantities, inventory levels, lead times, due dates, and other parameters.

Whereas the MPS produces an infinite capacity plan—a plan that does not consider your actual manufacturing capacity to fabricate the required products—the finite scheduling tool will use data from the MPS and/or from your production orders to plan according to production capacity. This feature is called smoothing. As a result, some production orders will be moved, probably delayed, to respect the plant's capacity to produce.

We rely on master production schedules (MPS), material resource planning (MRP), and finite scheduling because a computer can crunch numbers better than any human being. That being said, a computer cannot, even relying on artificial intelligence, give you accurate results with inaccurate data. To further emphasize this point, the literature states that your inventory precision must be 97 percent for material resource planning to be effective.

Using this functionality on a large volume of data requires good transactional discipline from all system users within the organization, but also the support of thorough and meticulous production planners. It is often difficult and time-consuming to find the reason behind error messages or to pinpoint a problem in the configurations and setups.

When used properly, production planning will help by giving you foresight. The net effect should be reduced inventory levels, shorter lead times, and fewer inventory shortages, saving you thousands or even hundreds of thousands of dollars. Keep in mind, however, that it is not transaction-based and thus probably the most difficult ERP business function to successfully exploit.

Case Study

After implementing production planning and running their system for four months, the company controller was incredulous to see that inventory levels were in fact increasing, not diminishing. How could that be possible? The software vendor had alluded to smaller inventories, and this whole phase of the project was sold on the return on investment this would provide. Sarah was getting nervous, so she decided to go meet with Charles, the production planner, to discuss the issue.

Charles assured her that the system was performing adequately and that the kinks they had first experienced had been ironed out. He was not sure why inventory levels were increasing. Sarah, who wanted to address this issue before it got out of hand, decided she would perform a physical count as soon as possible. With the help of operations, they scheduled the next count, but to her dismay, it could not be performed until six months after go-live.

Fast-forward to the physical-count weekend.

Sarah had the reports in hand, and she was analyzing the results. Although the value of her stock had decreased a bit this past month, it was still higher than normal. She was determined to get to the bottom of this. That's when she noticed that the slow movers from the last end-of-year physical count were all pretty much still there, but she also had more of the materials they used intensively. Charles had also mentioned that they had experienced less disturbance in production runs in the last couple of months due to shortages. That's when it hit her.

Inventory levels were increasing because they were stocking more of what they really needed while not yet having been able to fully utilize what they seldomly required. This was a normal transitional period. She would keep a close eye on things but felt confident this asset would shrink to adequate proportions from month to month.

INTERNET OF THINGS

Modern technology has become a total phenomenon for civilization, the defining force of a new social order in which efficiency is no longer an option but a necessity imposed on all human activity.

—Jacques Ellul

Key Takeaway: The Internet of Things, objects exchanging data with one another, is a component of Industry 4.0, helping revolutionize manufacturing.

The Internet of Things (IoT) represents all objects and equipment that can communicate with one another over the Internet or some other network. These objects may include sensors, cameras, and software. According to David Maayan, there are essentially five types of IoT applications:

1. **Consumer IoT**—such as an intelligent home or an appliance that lets you know when it requires servicing
2. **Commercial IoT**—for example, vehicle-to-vehicle communication (V2V), security monitoring systems, or intelligent health devices
3. **Infrastructure IoT**—a form of object network that includes energy and asset management systems that can be used in smart cities
4. **Military Things (IoMT)**—can be surveillance robots, human-wearable biometrics, equipment-tracking devices, among others

5. **Industrial (IIoT)**—used to improve productivity by enhancing automation and providing data from which better decisions can be made, (for example, smart agriculture)

Within the context of manufacturing, IIoT—with cloud computing, big data, and artificial intelligence—is referred to as Industry 4.0. These technologies are progressively transforming production facilities. I recently attended an event in which these technologies were favored to revolutionize the mining industry.

Artificial intelligence and big data are covered in the next chapter.

So what is the relationship between IoT and your ERP system? The latter system supports and integrates all your operations. An IoT network deployed in your manufacturing plant will provide great data to support your manufacturing processes. Some of that data will be closely related to your machines and equipment and thus may not seem very valuable for the people using your ERP system.

The rest of that data, however, can be extremely interesting. If you interface your ERP system with your IoT network, you can improve the automation of your operations. For example, whenever your machine produces a gizmo, information such as quantity and quality parameters can be sent to your ERP system in real time, thus generating an automatic output transaction, immediately materializing your inventory.

You could also cross-reference data between your ERP solution and your IoT data warehouse to help with business intelligence—joining financial data with manufacturing data for better insight and decision-making.

The primary benefits of integrating ERP with IoT are the following:

1. Better decision-making

2. Real-time business insights
3. Improved asset management
4. Greater operational efficiency
5. Improved forecasting

As Brendan O'Brien puts it, "If you think the Internet has changed your life, think again. The Internet of Things is about to change it all over again!"

Case Study

Since we have not yet worked with IoT, our case study is one published by Microsoft. Fischerwerke specializes in fixing and fastening technologies. Among their product offering, we find sensors connected to Azure IoT.

These sensors help engineers and workers determine the load that a particular bolt on a structure may be burdened with. Alerts can be sent if that load reaches a critical threshold.

Moreover, constant monitoring of the various fasteners on a structure can provide predictive data, improving maintenance and security.

SECTION 8
DIGITAL AGE

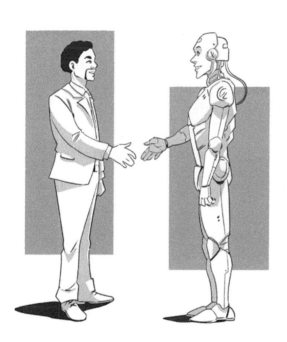

BIG DATA AND AI

Before we work on artificial intelligence why don't
we do something about natural stupidity?

—Tom Chatfield

> **Key Takeaway: Even though you may not realize
> it, you are already using big data and artificial
> intelligence. Be ready for more.**

According to Wikipedia, big data primarily refers to data sets—
sometimes structured, sometimes not—that are too large or
complex to be dealt with by traditional data-processing application
software. Big data harbors the following five characteristics:
volume, value, variety, velocity, and veracity.

We currently have the hardware capability to store unimaginable
amounts of data. Disk space is cheap, and cloud computing is
growing exponentially. Combine this with our ability to gather data
using IoT and other means, and you end up with more information
than the human brain can comprehend. *(Considering I can hardly
remember what I had for breakfast yesterday, you might say it isn't
such a big leap forward, but trust me, we are a loooong way past
512MB hard drives.)*

Microsoft provides an example of how big data can be used in
the ERP realm. They gather navigation telemetry from their cloud
offerings to see how users utilize their solutions. This gives them
valuable insight to improve user experience by streamlining
navigation, reducing input errors, and other user pitfalls they find.

As mentioned, big data can be valuable if interpreted correctly and quickly enough. This is where artificial intelligence comes in. The *Oxford Dictionary* defines *artificial intelligence* as "the theory and development of computer systems able to perform tasks that normally require human intelligence, such as visual perception, speech recognition, decision-making, and translation between languages." IBM defines it simply as "a field which combines computer science and robust datasets to enable problem-solving."

So where do you find big data? Government agencies and companies offer some of their data for free! Some examples are the following:

1. **Data.gov**—this US government site acts as a portal to information on everything from climate to crime.
2. **Amazon Web Services Public Datasets**—these include the 1000 Genomes Project.
3. **Google Trends** provides statistics on searches.
4. **Freebase** is a community-compiled database of structured data about people, places, and things.

Big data and AI have a synergistic relationship. AI requires a massive amount of data to learn, interpret, derive patterns, and improve decision-making. Big data is good at gathering said data but is not able to process it. Big data provides the fuel for AI.

Artificial intelligence is being leveraged in ERP systems. Some tasks can be difficult to accomplish by conventional means, and this is where AI can help. Below are some examples of AI applications in ERP systems.

Cash-flow Forecasting

You can predict your company's cash flow based on information such as sales orders, purchase orders, payables, receivables, and cash on hand. This may provide insight into the next two or three months. You need a crystal ball to see beyond the future data you possess.

Using IA, however, you can consider the last three years of history and identify payment patterns—for example, customers that historically don't pay on time—that can impact the future of your business. You may also be able to extrapolate sales based on past performance and therefore obtain a better prediction of future cash influx.

Production Planning

This ability AI has to discern patterns may help demand forecasting, production planning, and transportation management. Your master production schedule can literally become more intelligent if given enough good data to process.

Automation

Various automation tasks can further be improved with the use of AI. Customers may be able to *chat* with your system to generate orders. Your system could detect a piece of equipment that is about to overheat and create a maintenance work order to address the issue.

Coding

We recently tested Microsoft's Copilot to see if it could generate AL programming. AL code is the programming language used to write Business Central. We found out that Copilot can generate snippets of code if the instructions you provide are clear enough. It is not perfect, but it can help a developer save time, especially when working on something new. Instead of spending hours searching for information on how to use a specific function, for example, you can just ask Copilot to write the code for you.

Artificial intelligence is in the news as I write this chapter. ChatGPT is trying to draw hands properly, and students are learning to use AI to cheat. This can be overwhelming. Arthur C. Clarke said it best: "Any sufficiently advanced technology is indistinguishable from magic." *(By the way, Copilot in Word is helping me write this by automatically completing words as I type them. We'll be sooo lazy soon.)*

Case Study

We asked BingChat to give us a balanced definition of artificial intelligence. Questions to BingChat can be precise, balanced, or creative. This is the answer we obtained, sources included:

Artificial intelligence (AI) is the ability of a digital computer or computer-controlled robot to perform tasks commonly associated with intelligent beings.[2] These tasks include speech recognition, decision-making, visual perception, and translation between languages[3]. AI is a field that combines computer science and robust datasets to enable problem-solving.[4] It also encompasses sub-fields of machine learning and deep learning.[5]

We then asked BingChat if it can think like a human. To which it replied:

---

[2] Conversation with Bing, 2023-05-17(1) Artificial intelligence - Wikipedia. https://en.wikipedia.org/wiki/Artificial_intelligence Accessed 2023-05-17.

[3] What is Artificial Intelligence (AI) ? | IBM. https://www.ibm.com/topics/artificial-intelligence Accessed 2023-05-17.

[4] https://bing.com/search?q=what+is+artificial+intelligence%3f Accessed 2023-05-17.

[5] Artificial intelligence (AI) | Definition, Examples, Types .... https://www.britannica.com/technology/artificial-intelligence Accessed 2023-05-17.

I cannot think like a human because I do not have the same cognitive abilities or experiences as humans. I can only perform tasks that are programmed by humans or learned from data. I can try to imitate human behavior, but I do not understand the meaning or context behind it.

BUSINESS INTELLIGENCE

It is not the strongest of the species that survives,
nor the most intelligent, but the one most responsive
to change.

—Charles Darwin

> **Key Takeaway: Business intelligence gathers data
> and presents it in a way that it becomes action-
> able information.**

According to IBM, business intelligence (BI) is *software that ingests business data and presents it in user-friendly views such as reports, dashboards, charts, and graphs.*

Most definitions of business intelligence you can find on the Internet mention data, analytics, and making decisions, or variations thereof. I must insist, however, on the user-friendly keywords that are in IBM's abovementioned definition. Even though some aspects of business intelligence can be very complex, the targeted result is to present information in a format that is both simple and valuable to the user, which is why we often see the product of business intelligence as visual dashboards.

The data being used by BI software, such as Microsoft Power BI, can come from various sources, including your ERP system. This data is often saved in a repository called a data warehouse. Using a data warehouse is particularly helpful because the volume of data that is being stored and analyzed is often too large to rely on your ERP system for that purpose.

Moreover, your ERP database is configured and tuned for online transaction processing (OLTP) while business intelligence relies on online analytical processing (OLAP) databases to run efficiently. The difference between the two is technical and has to do with how the format of the data used for reporting differs from the format required by ERP systems.

An OLTP database is typically built to accept large volumes of short, recurring transactions: writing, modifying, or deleting records of information. An OLTP database is a sprinter.

OLAP databases are designed to accept large volumes of information, more or less structured, that will also be analyzed in large volumes. Multiple records will be created when the data warehouse is populated, perhaps nightly, and large amounts of data will be queried—in other words, retrieved—when reports or dashboards are generated. An OLAP database is a marathoner.

You can use the data directly from your ERP system to produce business intelligence dashboards, but it may impact your other users when performing their daily duties such as adding customers, generating orders, consuming inventory, etc. The number of users, transactional volume, and size of your database will dictate how long this approach remains viable.

Once you have defined your data sources and want to leverage business intelligence in your company, you must determine what key information is required to make better decisions. This information will most likely be shown as graphs and charts in a dashboard because the information is only helpful if it can be easily and quickly interpreted and acted upon. These visual tools are normally based on key performance indicators.

FinancesOnline defines KPIs as the following:

The KPIs in business intelligence are typically around major business areas such as financial metrics, marketing metrics, customer service metrics, and HR metrics. KPIs also cover specific areas like project management metrics and retail metrics. These KPIs are measurable outcomes that indicate the company's performance against its goals. To define your KPIs for successful business intelligence, you have to identify which aspects of your business you want to look into and have all the relevant data in your hand. Investing in a powerful business intelligence tool should let you calculate your KPIs faster, with many of them capable of diving deep into your data and generating novel insights to inform your next decisions and actions.

A good business intelligence tool will allow you to filter, sort, and drill down into the data to better understand the driving factors behind a KPI, often pointing to some issue. Indeed, business intelligence enables management by exception (MBE), which, according to Wikipedia, focuses on identifying and handling cases that deviate from the norm.

Below is a Power BI example captured on zoomcharts.com:

Business intelligence is often deployed to leverage your own data, especially when you first get started. You can, however, include big data in your business intelligence strategy provided you have the right tools to do so. For instance, by using a premium capacity, Power BI will handle trillions of rows and petabytes of data. (Petabytes? Is that some new brand of dog food?) A petabyte holds 1,024 terabytes of data!

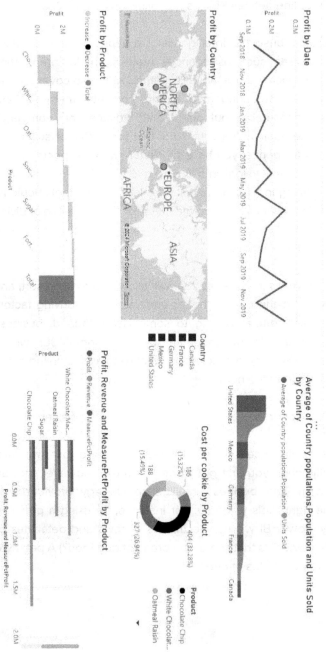

Performance Report

Case Study

As a benefit of deploying an ERP system, we recently designed a Power BI dashboard for one of our customers. This dashboard retrieves data from the manufacturing module and provides immediate performance insight. That insight was only previously available after tedious calculations and manipulations.

I am told the company's general manager was flabbergasted when she realized she would be able to consult this information daily.

BLOCKCHAIN

Knowledge is power. Information is power. The secreting or hoarding of knowledge or information may be an act of tyranny camouflaged as humility.
—Robin Morgan

> **Key Takeaway: A new technology, blockchain should gradually enhance ERP security and data integrity.**

Blockchain is well-known for its application with cryptocurrency, but it can be used in different contexts. In layman's terms, a blockchain is a shared, distributed database where each data element is linked to the previous element, authenticated, and once saved, cannot be altered. Instead of storing a transaction ledger on your local server, using blockchain, you can store it on multiple computers, thereby improving its integrity against hackers, data theft, and corruption.

Applying blockchain technology to ERP systems could help publicly sharing data such as lot tracking or supply chain information. Imagine being able to trace a manufactured lot from its birth even before you bought it, received it, and created it in your own ERP. In other words, taking traceability outside the boundaries of your own system.

Perhaps you'd like to know where the goods you purchased are right now and when they will arrive, and you'd like to have them scanned into your inventory without the help of human intervention.

Blockchain will improve integration between multiple, previously estranged systems, effectively enhancing collaboration between business partners. Visibility of nonconfidential data will be raised by sharing it across a blockchain network accessible to all parties involved.

Another potential application is related to smart contracts. International trading, for example, could be improved by tracking the goods as they transit to your warehouse, but also automatically initiating the transfer of funds when all predefined quality and trading rules are met. This would create a safer transaction for all parties involved.

Case Study

This case study is not an event I have experienced myself but an endeavor Walmart Canada has pioneered to fix recurring logistics problems with its carrier.

Before the application of blockchain, discrepancies in the invoice and payment process would cause delays and require much effort to reconcile.

This is an excellent real-life example of blockchain put to good use. You can read the full article titled "How Walmart Canada Uses Blockchain to Solve Supply-Chain Challenges" on the Harvard Business Review *website.[6]*

Although the article doesn't specify it, I am convinced their blockchain network integrates with their ERP solution.

---

[5] https://hbr.org/2022/01/how-walmart-canada-uses-blockchain-to-solve-supply-chain-challenges

CONCLUSION

The only thing more expensive than education is ignorance.

—Benjamin Franklin

> **Key Takeaway: Knowledge and preparation are your allies.**

We have skimmed the surface of most topics presented in this book so you would know enough to keep up with ERP vendors and professionals, understand their jargon, and develop some critical ability to discern truths and falsehoods.

Despite the technological aspects, the challenges encountered in ERP projects are still very much about people, not bits and bytes. Preparation and proper management remain key to improving your probability of success.

I really hope reading this second edition of my book has proven helpful. I feel that this version is much improved and, of course, up to date. Technology evolves at such a disconcerting pace it's hard to keep up. I wonder if a third edition might be entirely written by artificial intelligence. *(In which case, of course, there would be no humor. And if there is, it won't be funny.)*

It is also my desire that the additional content provided in www. erphelp.co/downloadables can also be of help.

Thanks for reading my book. I welcome suggestions and positive feedback. *(Adulation, money donations, and firstborns—if they are old enough to work—are also appreciated.)*

Cheers!

BIBLIOGRAPHY

Beaubouef, Grady Brett. "Applying Pareto's Principle to ERP Selections." ERP the Right Way!, October 18, 2010. https://erptherightway.com/2010/10/18/applying-paretos-principle-to-erp-selection-projects/.

"Benefits of Big Data, AI, and Advanced Analytics." Qlik, May 17, 2022. https://www.qlik.com/us/augmented-analytics/big-data-ai.

Campbell, Christine, "Pros and Cons of blockchain for ERP." TechTarget, June 9, 2023. https://www.techtarget.com/searchcio/tip/Pros-and-cons-of-blockchain-for-ERP.

Cherry, Kendra. "Self-Determination Theory and Motivation." Edited by David Susman, PhD. Verywell Mind, November 8, 2022. https://www.verywellmind.com/what-is-self-determination-theory-2795387.

Clayton, Mike. "12 Project Planning Mistakes . . . And How to Fix Them." Online PM Courses, November 20, 2017. https://onlinepmcourses.com/project-planning-mistakes/.

Dent, Eric B., and Susan Galloway Goldberg. "Challenging 'Resistance to Change.'" *The Journal of Applied Behavioral Science* 35, no. 1 (March 1999): 25–41. https://doi.org/10.1177/0021886399351003.

Fowler, Susan. *Why Motivating People Doesn't Work . . . And What Does*. Berrett-Koehler Publishers, 2014.

"Hardfacts on Software - the 12 Cardinal Sins of ERP Implementation." *Namibia Economist*, November 11, 2011. https://economist.com.na/103/columns/hardfacts-on-software-the-12-cardinal-sins-of-erp-implementation/#:~:text=Surveys%20have%20shown%20that%20inadequate.

"Integrating ERP with IoT—What Are the Benefits?" IT Convergence (blog), October 21, 2019. https://www.itconvergence.com/blog/5-benefits-of-integrating-erp-with-iot-technology/.

Leon, Alexis. *ERP Demystified*. 3rd ed. New Delhi: Mcgraw-Hill Education, 2014.

Maayan, Gilad David. "The IoT Rundown for 2020: Stats, Risks, and Solutions—Security Today." *Security Today*, January 13, 2020. https://securitytoday.com/articles/2020/01/13/the-iot-rundown-for-2020.aspx.

Miller, Chris. "Business Intelligence Key Performance Indicators (KPIs) with Examples." Financesonline.com, May 14, 2019. https://

financesonline.com/business-intelligence-key-performance-indicators-kpis-with-examples/.

Montanino, Paolino. "Artificial Intelligence and the Evolution of ERP Systems." LinkedIn, June 8, 2022. https://www.linkedin.com/pulse/artificial-intelligence-evolution-erp-systems-paolino-montanino/.

Segal, Troy. "Big Data." Investopedia, November 29, 2022. https://www.investopedia.com/terms/b/big-data.asp.

"10 Business Process Modelling Techniques Explained, with Examples." GetSmarter with EdX (blog), August 7, 2020. https://www.getsmarter.com/blog/career-advice/10-business-process-modelling-techniques/.

"The 2016 ERP Report." Panorama Consulting Group, 2016. https://www.panorama-consulting.com/resource-center/erp-report-archives/.

"Understanding How Forces Act: Azure IoT Helps Fischer Carry out Continuous Structural Monitoring and Thus Enhance Safety." Microsoft Customers Stories, May 3, 2023. https://customers.microsoft.com/en-ca/story/1625853849434740413-fischer-azure-azureiot-en.

www.ingramcontent.com/pod-product-compliance
Lightning Source LLC
Chambersburg PA
CBHW071239050326
40690CB00011B/2191